Praise for Ki and **I AM STRONG!**

Kirk's formula helps readers get out of their own way to discover that they are strong and completely worthy of greatness, love, success, and joy!

> **Michelle May, M.D.,** author of *Eat What You Love, Love What You Eat*

The principles in this book changed my life! I have overcome self doubt and feel more confident, capable and worthy of my true purpose than I have felt in a long, long time. I now face life once again without fear and with renewed hope for the future. Want to feel better about yourself and your future? Read this book!

> **Sandi Ashton** – Writer, Business Coach, Managing Director Career Connectors

"I adore Kirk Wilkinson. His incredible story of overcoming cancer and reconnecting with an awareness of how to choose to be happy in the most difficult of times provided a remarkable road map in his first book, *The Happiness Factor*. In *I am Strong!*, Kirk inspires all of us with a simple formula for finding our inner strength, for reconnecting with our true sense of self-worth, and for actively changing the course of our lives by taking back control over our emotions and choices. We all have to do hard things in our lives; we all have to learn how to move forward on our truest and most inspired path even when presented with what seems like insurmountable challenges. Kirk Wilkinson talks to the deepest reaches of our souls and calls out the incredible courage that resides there, showing us how to succeed and be truly, wildly strong in every sense of the word."

> **Tara Meyer-Robson,** Creator of The Flow Method and award-winning author of *The Flow: 40 Days to Total Life Transformation*

This well written guide book is filled with helpful and useful information. My favorite segments were the use of acronyms. Kirk uses truly compelling stories, some of which were so meaningful I read them a second time. He uses analogies to make his points in a sensitive and thoughtful way; and the book is chock full interesting self assessments. Whether you're currently living with abuse, like many of the clients I work with, or have some other difficulty in your past or current life, you'll find this book meaningful.

> **Stephanie Angelo,** SPHR, President, Human Resource Essential, LLC a multiple award-winning expert in domestic violence's effects on the workplace and author of *Serrated – A True Story of Survival, Recovery and the Pursuit of Justice.*

I absolutely love Kirk Wilkinson's book, *I Am Strong!*. The reader is immediately drawn into the book because it meets you in that down to earth true to life place that most of us live. That said, it then steadily begins building your self-appraisal by practically illustrating how we allow ourselves to lose the lust and luster for life that we were born with.

Finally, by offering genuine options the reader gains the advantage of some remarkable alternatives to the old "tried and didn't work" ways of living.

The result is a metamorphous not unlike the chrysalis necessary for the caterpillar to fly.

> **Eldon Taylor** - NY Times bestselling author of *Choices and Illusions and Mind Programming* and Talk Radio Host: Provocative Enlightenment

Kirk

I AM STRONG!

The Formula to
Build your Self-Worth
and Discover your True Purpose
from the Inside Out!

Kirk Wilkinson

THE HAPPINESS FACTOR

I AM STRONG: The Formula to Build your Self-worth and Discover your True Purpose from the Inside Out!
Published by The Happiness Factor, 2011
Mesa, Arizona

Copyright © 2011 by Kirk Wilkinson
All rights reserved

Includes bibliographical references
ISBN 978-1-4507-7192-4

Cover design and typesetting by Susan Veach
Edited by Erin Martineau, Refiners Eye LLC
Illustrations by Tony Montano

Printed and bound in the United States of America. All rights reserved. No part of this book may be reproduced in any form or by any electronic or mechanical means including information storage and retrieval systems without permission in writing from the copyright holder, except by a reviewer who may quote brief passages in review.

The scanning, uploading and distribution of this book via the Internet or via any other means without the permission of the publisher is illegal and punishable by law. Please purchase only authorized electronic editions, and do not participate in or encourage electronic piracy of copyrighted materials. Your support of the author's rights is appreciated.

To all those who need to know just how great, wonderful, marvelous and capable you are. You can be strong – you can do hard things!

Contents

I AM STRONG!

Acknowledgements

Words are not adequate to express my heartfelt thanks to my clients who have put their trust in me to be their guide for a short period in their lives to help them learn the skills that enabled them to save their marriages, overcome painful memories of the past and develop courage to create the lives they have always wanted. To respect their privacy and confidentiality, I have used pseudonyms in the various examples contained in this book. It is truly a tremendous feeling to be a part of someone's life as they embrace the I AM STRONG formula and transform their life.

I am also grateful for the many opportunities I have had to fine-tune the sections in this book through live seminars, workshops and keynote presentations. I first approached Nancy Cook, Director of Spiritual Care for Mercy Gilbert and Chandler Regional Hospitals near Phoenix, Arizona. Nancy had both an open mind and open heart to see the potential of this material to change the lives of hospital employees and volunteers through the *Living with Purpose* series.

Additionally, I am grateful to Erin Martineau of RefinersEye.com who is so much more than a skilled and artful editor. She contributes in such a way that I am able to focus more on the content and examples, knowing she will make sure you, as the reader, have a better experience with this book.

Lastly, I am grateful to my wife Karen of 32 years not only for her love and ongoing support but also for her journey of overcoming severe depression and anxiety and realizing that she, too, is a strong woman, capable of doing hard things.

Introduction

"I just don't know who I am anymore!" Cara said. "I have given so much of myself at my job, and also as a mother, wife, caregiver, housekeeper, and taxi driver to my children that I feel as if I have lost myself and don't know who I am." Too many of you, like Cara, have told me the same thing in coaching sessions. Many of you have faced divorce, rejection, financial setbacks, emotional and physical abuse, and hardships that have derailed, hurt and altered you to such an extent that you no longer recognize or like the person you see in the mirror.

In another recent conversation, Terri, a 37-year-old mother of three, told me that she felt lost and confused. Four years ago her world turned upside down when her husband of 10 years left her. Her self-esteem met an all-time low, and she turned to me for help. Terri explained that the vibrant, beautiful, capable woman she thought she was had been replaced by an insecure, fearful, timid woman whom she barely recognized. As a single mother trying to make ends meet, she felt constant guilt over having to miss much of her children's lives. She felt that she was giving so much of herself to her job and others that there was nothing left to make her feel 'whole.' "Is there any hope for me?" Terri asked. "I don't know how much longer I can do this!"

Don't think that this is a condition experienced only by women.

Jack, 42, feels as if life is passing him by. He expected by this point in his life to be making more money, to have a better relationship with his wife, to have a better position at work and to be more confident. He had applied for more than 200 jobs, only to be rejected each time. He feels worthless and as if his true identity has abandoned him. It has been hard for him to admit that he is suffering from a serious mid-life crisis made worse by losing his job. Having to settle for a job for which he is overqualified makes him feel even more insecure, unworthy and lost.

I have heard many, many similar stories in one-on-one sessions with clients or talking with individuals after seminars. Through my vocation as a life-coach, public speaker, and author, I have found that feelings of rejection, worthlessness, under-appreciation, and a general lack of self-love, self-respect and lost identity are more common than I had previously imagined. If this describes you, then you are in luck because this book and the accompanying audio and video courses are designed especially for you. By applying the principles and skills presented in this book, you CAN and WILL rediscover who you are, grow your self-worth and self-esteem, overcome negative past experiences, forgive those who have hurt you, begin to live a life with purpose, and learn how to feel joy, even true pleasure, every day. You may be thinking that you have tried other self-help books and courses, and it was just too hard to stick with them to get the promised results. Don't be discouraged! YOU CAN DO HARD THINGS. YOU ARE STRONG!

Yes! You are strong! No matter what you have experienced in the past, no matter what you are faced with at this very moment, you can make it. You can do hard things! Whether you felt confident at one time in your life and no longer feel that way or have never felt confident and worthy of success and happiness, this book is meant for you. Read on and learn the formula to build your self-worth, obtain emotional freedom, experience your inherent potential, and live your true life's purpose. Unburden yourself of the emotional baggage that is holding you back and live the life you are meant to live! This is not a fantasy; this is not a fairy tale. You can do this, and this book and the accompanying courses will provide you with a formula that has been tried and tested in workshops, seminars and in hundreds of one-on-one sessions with my clients. In fact, each section in this book comes directly from live seminars that have been taught around the world. Do your best to suspend judgment, skepticism and uncertainty, and proceed with the faith that as you implement the practical and real-world skills covered in this book, you will soon feel your self-worth grow; you will emerge as a more confident individual, and you will know your true life purpose. The most immediate benefit you will obtain is that you will actually begin to feel free from insecurities and emotional baggage, and you will be happy! You will feel the power that comes from being strong!

The I AM STRONG formula described in the first two parts of this book is essential to your success. Feeling truly worthy of happiness, success, satisfaction and fulfillment will lead you to a desire to forgive, to overcome your negative past, to discover your true life's purpose and experience deep joy.

To get started, consider this question: if you could be anyone – who would you be? Think about this question for a moment and take it seriously. If you could be anyone, anybody at all, who would you be? This is not a trick question. Perhaps you would choose to be someone who has touched your heart or inspired you in some way. Maybe it is your favorite celebrity or sports icon. It might even be your father or mother or another family member whom you respect and admire. When I have asked this question in a corporate setting, people sometimes mention the name of their first manager or supervisor, a high school teacher or college professor.

The most appropriate answer to this question is, "I am happy being me!" This is exactly what this book hopes to achieve – to empower you to be able to sincerely answer that you are happy just being YOU! You are a powerful, wonderful, capable, talented, gifted human being. That, in essence, is the power of the I AM STRONG formula – to build your self-worth and enable you to discover your true purpose in life so that you can experience joy on a daily basis. If you feel that the goal of this book is too difficult, too lofty and unrealistic, please suspend your judgment and trust that this is not an impossible, but very likely and probable, outcome of this book.

Have you become someone you don't like? Have things happened to you that cause you to question your worth and value? No matter what has happened to you, you are capable of rediscovering your true potential and true self-worth and living a life full of significance, blessings and miracles.

This book and the accompanying courses are organized into several parts:

1. I AM STRONG: The Formula
2. Build Your Self-Worth: The I AM STRONG Formula in Action
3. Receive the Miracles of Forgiving
4. Transform from Victim to Hero in 90 Seconds
5. Live Your Life with Purpose
6. Experience Joy and Happiness Every Day

Each section includes a self-assessment that you can use as you read or as you listen to the audio courses. The audio courses are recordings of the live workshops on each topic. Also accompanying this book is a series of short video segments that will help you implement the skills and practical tips. You can find a link to the audio and video courses and one of these websites: www.thehappinessfactor. com or www.IAMSTRONG.co.

Each section is meant to be interdependent, meaning that it is not requisite that you follow the sections in order, even though the principles build upon one another consecutively. If you are initially drawn to one section more than another, feel free to follow that inspiration and start with the section that you feel you need most. However, Parts 1 and 2 set the foundation for the rest, so I highly recommend that you begin with the first two parts to establish context.

A word of caution and a disclaimer: when I was in the same place as many of you are right now, I felt as if I would never be happy and that I was a failure at all the things that were important to me. I didn't have the job I wanted, my relationship with my wife was nowhere near what it should have been, my children were withdrawing from me, and my sense of self was diminishing. Wanting to change things, I set out trying to change my circumstances, my job, my spouse, my children, my house, my car, the city I lived in, and none of it worked. It wasn't until a friend said to me, "All of your problems will be solved from the inside out," that I finally got it. This book and the accompanying courses will focus on change from the inside out and not the other way around. I have tried to write this book as if you and I were speaking one-on-one with the goal to provide you with as many practical skills as I can without delving too much into the theoretical or rhetorical. I am also hoping to challenge you to look at yourself differently, to see yourself in a new light, to reclaim the person you truly are, rather than someone who is a victim to circumstance or the acts of others. You are capable, beautiful, wonderful and powerful. Claim your right to be great, rediscover your true potential and worth, and live a life of purpose. YOU ARE STRONG! YOU CAN DO HARD THINGS!

What You Will Learn

Part 1: The I A M S T R O N G Formula

This part provides an overview of the powerful formula to build your self-worth. The formula is embodied in the short statement: I AM STRONG. Consider Part 1 as an introduction to this powerful formula that will be put into action in Part 2. The I AM STRONG formula will help you learn how to draw the distinction between *who* you are and what you *do*, as well as how to distinguish between self-worth, self-esteem and self-confidence.

Part 2: The I A M S T R O N G Formula in Action

After learning the foundation and elements of the I AM STRONG formula, you can now put it into action with real-world practical skills that will impact every aspect of your life. These powerful skills include learning to create a criticism filter, silencing your inner critic, and standing up for your own feelings and emotions. You will not be the same after reading Part 2. You will actually feel worthy of success, true love and happiness.

Part 3: Authentic Forgiving

This part of the book is about learning how to forgive yourself and forgive those who have hurt or offended you. You authentically forgive when the forgiveness is done in the right way for the right reasons. You cannot give what you do not have; if you cannot give yourself the forgiveness you deserve, it will be that much harder to forgive others. One of the reasons you might feel lost after a divorce or rejection is that you are focused on the hurt instead of forgiving. Authentic forgiving is part of the healing process. In these chapters you will learn the steps to forgiving yourself and others and why it frees you from the emotional pain you have been carrying for a long time.

Part 4: From Victim to Hero in 90 Seconds

We have all had things happen to us in the past that we re-live as we tell ourselves the story about what happened. It is time to stop focusing on what happened and start focusing on what you have learned and how you have grown. In these chapters you will learn how to overcome being a victim of the past and become a hero in your own life story. You will experience a palpable freedom as you release the negativity of your past. You will be able to look to the future with hope and positive anticipation. The skills and principles in these chapters will enable you to go from being a victim to a hero in 90 seconds or less.

Part 5: Live Your Life with Purpose

There is nothing like the feeling of anticipating something positive around the corner. Too often we start living by default; life becomes something that just happens, and we feel as if we are riding a merry-go-round with no destination or purpose. Living each day without a purpose can feel like a prison sentence. It is time to escape the prison you have built for yourself and create a life of purpose that is significant and meaningful and affirms your worth and value. In these chapters you will learn what a true life purpose is and write your purpose so you can start to effectively live it.

Part 6: Experience Joy and Happiness Every Day

Very few experiences are either all bad or all good. Learn how to reset your positive experience set-point to recognize the positive in apparently negative experiences. I will discuss several joy-blockers and help you learn practical skills that increase your ability to feel positive and experience happiness every single day – even when things go wrong. Think of these chapters as the result of the I AM STRONG formula – experiencing the deep joy that life truly has to offer.

Becoming strong and developing the power to do hard things will come from creating a firm foundation of self-worth and reducing negative emotions that can weaken your self-worth and your ability to live a satisfying and fulfilling life. The chapters in this book will help you do just that. You will create a foundation of worth and then learn to use that foundation to eliminate emotional burdens that you are currently experiencing with the ultimate goal of living a joyful and happy life. You don't need to leave town to 'find yourself.' You don't need to spend a year traveling the world eating good food, learning to meditate in India or study ancient Chinese philosophy to find out who you are.

You are great. You are capable. YOU CAN DO HARD THINGS! No matter what you have done, no matter what has happened to you, no matter how old or how young you are, you can rediscover your true life purpose, feel worthy of happiness and fulfillment and reduce the negativity that comes into your life. Let me help you wake up to the real you, the wonderful you, the talented, capable, fantastic you!

In a very short time you will feel the strength you have been missing, and you will be able to say with confidence, "I AM STRONG!"

Part 1

The
I AM STRONG
Formula

I AM STRONG!

Deep down, all of us WANT to feel valued – and so we spend much of our lives striving for significance. We search for meaning in the things we do and the people we are with. We seek after significance in our jobs and in the various roles we play. That search can be draining and discouraging, and meaning and significance can seem so elusive. But here is a secret: you don't need to search any longer because the significance you are seeking and need is already within you!

In 1939, MGM released a movie that has since become one of the most watched movies of all time. The American Film Institute has rated this movie as one of the best films ever made. What is that movie? It is *The Wizard of Oz*. We all know the story featuring Dorothy and her misfit companions, the Tin Man, the Scarecrow, and the Cowardly Lion. Each of these characters is looking for something, and they search high and low to find it. But it isn't until near the end of the movie that we learn the irony of the story. The irony is that they already had what they were looking for. Dorothy already had the power to go home. The Tin Man already had a heart. The Scarecrow had a brain and the Cowardly Lion already had the courage he so greatly needed. You and I are like these characters, searching for what we need the most and trying to find it in the most unlikely places. Is it found in our jobs, our title, our relationships? Is it found in what we do? No, it is not!

Just like the characters in *The Wizard of Oz*, you don't need to be given your significance; you already have it. Let me be your guide to help you discover what you already have and learn how to put it into action. All the significance you are searching for, all the validation you need, all the worthiness you need will be created from inside you and can be accessed through the powerful and life-changing formula found in the next few chapters. This formula will help you build high self-worth as a foundation to improve every aspect of your life.

The formula is simple, yet powerful. It is found in the acronym, I AM STRONG. Each letter represents a step to true self-discovery and fulfillment.

The I AM STRONG formula will create enormous benefits in every aspect of your life. These benefits will begin to appear as you learn and put the principles and skills of the formula into action. Here are some of the benefits you can expect as you learn and use the I AM STRONG formula:

- You become optimistic!
- You will learn to like and love yourself.
- You will start to behave and act with a sense of purpose.
- You will forgive easier.
- You will be healthier.
- You will be wealthier.
- You will have better and more fulfilling relationships.
- You will respond better to medical treatments.
- You will cope and handle change better.
- Your self-esteem and your self-confidence will grow.
- You will truly believe that you are worthy of all that life has to offer → happiness, love, success, fulfillment.
- You will have a deep KNOWLEDGE that you make a difference in this world.

As in the story of *The Wizard of Oz*, there is some irony to this formula. The irony is that you are already strong! You are stronger than you realize. There are several studies that indicate that we typically think our trials are more difficult than they actually turn out to be. In these same studies it has been shown that after a traumatic experience, such as witnessing the train bombings in Madrid, or being diagnosed with breast cancer, people experience significant personal growth. The growth they experience includes greater courage, more compassion for others, increased spirituality and better relationships. Most of us have believed that we do indeed become stronger through adversity, and now there is a growing body of research that proves just that.[1]

If you allow it, your struggles can indeed be the best thing for you. With the help of this book, the 'time-to-benefit' will be accelerated, reducing the amount of time you have to suffer. You are capable of feeling completely worthy of greatness, love, success, fulfillment and true happiness. Yes, YOU ARE STRONG! Don't be discouraged if you don't feel it now. You will soon feel the power of a healthy and vibrant self-worth that will increase your self-esteem and build your self-confidence.

Chapter 1

The Formula

The I AM STRONG formula will create inner strength that comes from a strong sense of worthiness. You will feel inherently worthy of all of your dreams, all that you desire, including true and lasting happiness. As a result, you will experience greater self-esteem and greater confidence. What used to bother and offend you will no longer be an issue. You will find inner strength to handle change, adversity, and life's drama better. The I AM STRONG formula is a nine-step process built on true principles and practical skills that will enable you to shed feelings of low self-worth and see yourself as a wonderful, capable, strong person.

I is for Identify

Most of us don't spend a lot of time dwelling on the health of our self-worth. It is so easy to blame others for our lack of confidence and low self-esteem that we rarely take a good look at ourselves to realize that we are much more capable of defining our happiness and significance than we realize. In this step of the formula, you will identify the sources from which you have been deriving your value. By identifying the source of your value, you can become aware of how your search for significance may cause you to misbehave. This exercise is meant to help you understand that the only reliable source of value is yourself.

Your worth and value come from within you. You will begin to look at yourself differently to determine if you have been seeking value in ways that are insincere and unreliable.

A is for Acknowledge and Accept

Once you identify the source of your self-worth, it is important to become aware of what triggers your emotional responses and how you react in certain situations. You do this through a process of observing yourself, becoming aware, acknowledging with compassion, and practicing acceptance. Until you are able to accept yourself, your circumstances, your strengths and weakness without self-indictment, you remain in denial, unable to move forward. You cannot change what you do not acknowledge and accept. In this step you will begin to see yourself differently. You will begin to lose your dependence on others to build you up and validate you.

M is for Minimize Your Weaknesses and Maximize Your Strengths

It is unfortunate that we are much more acquainted with our weaknesses than our strengths, believing that our weaknesses far outweigh our strengths and talents. In this step of the formula, you will take the weaknesses you now accept and acknowledge and minimize them. You will recognize that you have strengths, talents and gifts and learn to maximize them.

S is for Self-Recognition

Your self-worth is on shaky ground if you are dependent on validation from others to affirm your worth. Validation from others is inconsistent and can often be insincere, as people will often tell you what you want to hear, rather than the truth. In this step, you will learn the power of self-recognition and self-validation in order to cure your dependence on others to feel valued and worthy.

T is for True to You

Low self-worth is often a result of not living a life of integrity and fear of being found out. This is exhibited by insecurity, low self-confidence, and not trusting your own decisions, intuition and needs. As your self-worth increases you will have more integrity, as well as more confidence to make and keep promises. You will feel more comfortable in new situations or when meeting new people.

R is for Respect Your Needs

We all have needs. For many of you, those needs come second to the needs and desires of others. Honoring both your desire to be of service to others and your need for self-care requires wisdom and balance. In order to be able to provide the most appropriate service to others, you must also learn to express your own needs, stop comparing yourself to others and become more assertive. This doesn't mean you will be unreasonable or become an emotional bully; rather, you will learn how to prioritize self-care.

O is for Own It!

Taking responsibility and accepting accountability for your own emotions, thoughts, feelings and behavior is a critical part of the I AM STRONG formula. As you become emotionally accountable, you stop blaming others, which allows you to rise above being a victim to become the owner of your life. The other amazing thing about owning your life is that you can learn from those you used to blame and become an even better person because of it.

N is for Nourish

Your self-worth is a living thing. Without consistent and positive nourishment, your self-worth will wither away like a plant without water. In this step you will learn the power and benefits of creating a criticism filter. You will learn how to preserve, protect and affirm your great worth.

G is for Genuine

Applying the previous eight steps of the I AM STRONG formula will give you new, more accurate views and beliefs about yourself. By aligning what you now believe about yourself with your thoughts and actions, you will begin to live authentically and with integrity. High self-worth requires you to be genuine. When you are genuine, you significantly reduce the inner conflict that is present with low-self worth. Being genuine is a wonderful benefit of high self-worth.

You *Are* Not What You *Do*

"You need to give yourself more credit," is what I said to Jacqueline in our very first session. She had just finished explaining to me that since her divorce four years ago, her ex-husband had attempted to reconcile at least six times and had proposed (yes, proposed to be re-married) four times, only to repeatedly back out. If the rejection from the divorce wasn't enough, she had to experience rejection over and over again, a choice that stemmed from her desire to do all she could to best benefit her children. She went on to tell me that, at one time, she had been a confident, capable, and enthusiastic wife, mother and business woman. Today, she sees herself as a "wimp, coward, a bad mother and a failure at trying to put things back together." Jacqueline added that her self-esteem had bottomed out and that she cries all the time and hates herself and her circumstances. My words to Jacqueline are the same words I would tell you, if you, too, feel that you have lost your confidence, self-esteem and suffer low self-worth: "You need to give yourself more credit!"

I meet many, many people who are so concerned about being viewed as conceited or prideful that they have become their own worst enemy and criticize anything and everything about themselves. Out of all of my clients, I have only had a few who would be considered as having a "big head." Stop worrying about how bad you are and start seeing how great you are.

With almost every client I have discovered that once we tackle issues of self-worth and self-esteem, they have much greater success handling the issues that they wanted to talk about in the first place. In many cases a client will come to me for help with their self-esteem, when, in fact, they don't have a self-esteem problem but more likely an issue that stems from low self-worth. For this reason I have put the subject of self-worth in the first part of this book. So much of the negativity we experience can be minimized by having a healthy self-worth and by understanding the difference between self-worth, self-esteem and self-confidence.

You see, we all start with a healthy self-worth, and it is not until we experience life that we start to get all sorts of negative messages that compromise our self-worth. As both adults and children we are bombarded with positive and negative messages every day from our parents, friends, teachers, the media and other sources. The reports I have read put the number of negative messages from TV and media alone to 5,000 negative impressions an hour and up to 25,000 a day. Add in the various messages we get from those around us and those we love, and it is overwhelmingly negative. The messages I received while growing up were both intense and conflicting. I had one parent telling me that I was great and that I could do anything I set my mind to, and another convincing me that I was a nobody, that I couldn't do anything right, and that I would never amount to anything. Fortunately, I had at least one parent saying something positive; I have met too many people who have had very little or no positive feedback. With all of the negative and conflicting feedback and messages we receive over time, we begin to mistakenly interpret that negativity as a reflection of our worth.

Imagine for a moment that I were to offer you a brand new, crisp, clean, never-been-used, $100 bill and ask you how much the bill is worth? I am sure you would be quick to answer that the bill is worth $100. You might add that it is worth 100 items at the Dollar Store (not including tax)! You may view it as worth some hours of your hard work. You could view its worth in terms of exchanging it to buy something of value to you. Most of us recognize the worth of $100. Now, just before I actually hand the bill to you, I quickly pull it back and crush it up in my hands and throw it to the floor and step on it. After I step on it, I kick it across the room and then pick it up again and criticize it by saying something you might hear from a parent or spouse or a boss, like, "You stupid $100 bill! How could you be so dumb! Can't you do anything right? You are useless!" I then spit on it, blow my nose on it, wrinkle it up and tear up the edges! Exasperated and out of breath, I now offer the bill to you as yours to keep. Would you take it? Would you actually accept the money, or would you turn away and reject my offer?

If you are like most people, you would still accept the bill, knowing that even though it is no longer in perfect shape, it is still worth $100. Even though the bill I am offering you is beat up and visibly in horrible condition, it is still worth $100. But that still isn't the point! *Which $100 bill are you?* Are you the crisp, clean, brand new, never-been-used $100 bill, or is your life better represented by the beat up, wrinkled, torn, criticized, spit-on $100 bill? If we are honest with ourselves, we would likely say that we have lived a life more representative of the beat-up $100 bill. We have all had our share of hard knocks, critics, let-downs, setbacks and disappointments. We have had more than our share of people who have kicked us when we were down and criticized us instead of building us up. All of this causes us to feel torn, wrinkled and beat up.

Yet, we look at others as if they are the crisp, clean, perfect $100 bill and think we are somehow worth less than they are because we've been beaten up! *The point is that we are all of immeasurable worth* simply by virtue of *being!* We are all of the same priceless worth. Your worth cannot be calculated in terms of money or fame or popularity. You are worth far more than $100, and nothing that happens to you should ever diminish your worth, the worth you give to yourself, your self-worth. No matter what has 'happened' to you, no matter what negative things you have experienced, you are inherently priceless.

Add to this the notion that you are much greater, more capable, stronger, smarter and more worthy of success and happiness *because* of what has happened to you, like a stone in a raging river that is polished over the years or the clay pot that becomes more useful and stronger by being burned in a furnace. Stop doing yourself the disservice of thinking that you are less than someone else, that you are unworthy of success or unworthy of love or that no one cares for you! You are worth more than $100; you are priceless, and it is time to give yourself the credit you are due! You need to give yourself more credit.

I AM STRONG!

Chapter 2

Understanding Self-Worth, Self-Esteem and Self-Confidence

In any discussion about self-worth, self-esteem and self-confidence, I am inevitably asked about the difference between them. After looking long and hard and reading several books and scientific studies, I have not found satisfying definitions. So rather than cite definitions that I don't wholly agree with, I would rather describe them by introducing you to what I call the Self-Worth Pyramid. As you can see in the graphic, self-worth is the largest component and can be considered the foundation of the pyramid. Self-confidence is

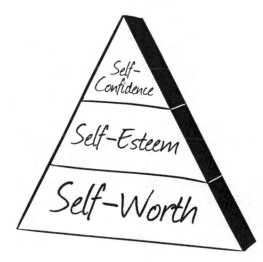

the smallest component and can be found at the top. Self-confidence is important and should not be disregarded, but it has less importance and significance than self-worth and self-esteem.

Self-worth is about *who you are* and is determined by your sense of being inherently worthy of happiness, worthy of reaching your potential, and worthy of fulfillment and satisfaction with all that life has to offer. It has strong personal significance and is mostly an internal phenomenon. You are considered as having high self-worth when you have a deep knowledge that by just being here you make a difference and that your life is having a positive impact on the world around you. This is not determined by anything external such as compliments and accolades. It is an internal knowledge of *who you are,* regardless of your external circumstances.

Those who enjoy high self-worth:

- Have quiet confidence and security in themselves.
- Have no need to prove themselves to others.
- Are comfortable with silence and comfortable alone.
- Do not fish for compliments - but they do accept them well.
- Demonstrate humility.
- Listen well to others.
- Recognize others and give credit where credit is due.
- Value external recognition second to internal satisfaction.

Self-worth emanates from the inside out. In addition to the above characteristics, you may also be able to observe that people with high self-worth appear to be physically relaxed, upright, calm and measured in movement. They are decisive, without hesitation. They make good eye contact freely and comfortably. We are naturally attracted to people with high self-worth because they make us feel comfortable, safe and secure.

Because self-worth is about *who you are* and not about *what you do,* it is important to understand that high self-worth is not about

I AM STRONG!

What you do

```
        /\
       /  \
      /Self-\
     /Confidence\
    /_____\
   /              \
  /   Self-Esteem   \
 /_____\
/                    \
/    Self-Worth        \
/_____\
```

Who you are — personal significance

feeling you deserve a reward for good behavior. It is about creating a foundation of value that is so strong that you are able to handle any upset, any adversity or challenge that comes your way and remain emotionally whole. In other words, you have emotional resourcefulness. Feeling worthy is different from feeling you deserve recognition, reward or validation. The word *deserve* represents some form of reciprocation: you do something and, therefore, deserve or have earned something in return. When you feel that you deserve something, you feel that you are owed some benefit or recognition because you have done something good, have sacrificed something or suffered in some way. Sometimes you may feel you deserve something merely because others have something you want too. Self-worth and feeling worthy are not about deserving anything; healthy self-worth is having a feeling or knowledge that you are unconditionally worthy of love, respect, happiness, success and fulfillment. It is a strong sense that you are inherently worthy just because of *who* you are.

We are bombarded with messages convincing us that we are entitled to greatness, good things, big cars, big houses or some kind of accolade because of something we *do*. Some people are only willing to serve others or will only feel good about having served others as long as they are recognized and acknowledged in some way. High self-worth does not demand recognition, it does not require accolades. High self-worth is a strong sense of *self* based on an internal 'knowing' that you are good, that you are valued, that you are worthy, even if no one says so.

Self-worth is strongly associated with your beliefs, particularly what you believe about yourself. While self-worth is not about your achievements, it drives you to spend energy and effort in pursuits that are meaningful to you. When you feel worthy, you feel motivated to make behavior choices that support your overall goals of success and joy. Self-worth should be a baseline of worthiness that can never diminish based on your situation or external circumstances. Later in this book I will share several things you can start to do right now to create a foundation of self-worth that cannot shrink but will only grow.

Self-confidence, on the other hand, is about *what you do* and is mostly developed from external sources, such as compliments, achievements and positive feedback. It is a by-product of self-worth and self-esteem, and it is dependent on situations and circumstances. For instance, I feel much more confident speaking in front of an audience when I have a fresh haircut. Perhaps you have experienced this as well when you wore your favorite dress or best suit for a job interview. Maybe you have experienced greater confidence when you prepared or practiced well for a performance. My wife is a musician, and I know she feels more confident when she has adequately practiced. You see, self-confidence is about *what you do*.

How you feel about what you can do is an external factor of how you feel about yourself. Not long ago I attempted to fulfill a life-long dream of learning to play the piano. It was fortunate that there was a willing teacher in our neighborhood. As I began to learn piano, I found that it was both easier and more difficult than I had anticipated!

Learning the notes came quickly to me. But getting the timing and rhythm right was challenging. When it came time for a recital, I was beside myself with a nervousness that completely surprised me. I am generally at home in front of an audience and quite confident in my ability to speak and convey a message. However, when it came to playing the piano in front of others, it was quite the opposite. As you can see, my self-confidence varies based on the circumstances, as I am sure yours does as well. This is in contrast to self-worth, which is not circumstantial and should not change with the situation.

I have found that many people focus foremost on building their self-confidence and then complain that they are not getting the results they had hoped for. The reason is that there is only so much gain you can get from improving your self-confidence. That is especially true if you have not taken the time to establish true self-worth, nor grown your self-esteem. Don't get me wrong. Self-confidence is important and should not be trivialized. But the small triangle at the top of the pyramid represents the limited return on investment you get from increased self-confidence.

Self-esteem is between self-confidence and self-worth and can best be described as thoughts and beliefs about what you can do because of who you are. Esteem is defined as an estimation of value; thus, self-esteem is your own estimation of your own value or worth. In essence, it is your own assessment of how worthy you feel. The problem with self-esteem is that we often measure our value using the wrong yardstick. Unfortunately, we have been taught that in order to be worthy of success or happiness we must have certain things. But worthiness has nothing to do with what you have; it is all about who you are. Self-esteem is not something you were born with; it is something you have learned. In fact, growing your self-esteem has more to do with un-learning low self-esteem behaviors than it does about learning how to have high self-esteem. Later in this part of the book you will learn a few skills that will help you un-learn low self-esteem behaviors.

Investing in your self-worth will produce direct beneficial results on your self-esteem and your self-confidence. It is so important to distinguish self-confidence, which is about *WHAT YOU DO*, from self-worth, which is about *WHO YOU ARE*, because too often we confuse the two – and that can wreak havoc on our well-being. For instance, when we are criticized about something we have 'done,' it is easy to interpret it as a criticism of *who we are*. I am sure that many of you have had a child who brought home a report card with lower grades than your child was capable of achieving. What was your reaction? I am sure you avoided the temptation to call your child dumb or stupid because you realize that the number-one reason for a bad grade is not your child's intelligence. What is the number one reason for a bad grade? Lack of effort! Most often a bad grade is a reflection of effort. You may have then tried to help your child realize that in order to get good grades he may need to put in more effort; yet, it turned into a fight or argument – why? Because your child, like many of us have done in the same situation, confused something they have *DONE* with *WHO THEY ARE*. Your words communicate that more effort is needed to get good grades; but what your child may be hearing is that they are not smart enough.

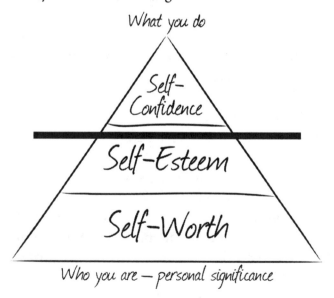

Even as adults we do the same thing. I have seen this over and over again with my clients when they interpret criticism and rejection as demeaning who they are – letting the negative comments flow down into the bottom of the pyramid – instead of keeping it at the top of the pyramid and letting it be about something they have done. We need to realize and help our children to realize the distinction between something we *do* and who we *are*.

Steve came to my office determined that he was a bad person. He asked me to help him overcome his issues with self-confidence. After some discussion I learned that Steve had completely reversed his notions of self-worth and self-confidence. He certainly was not a bad person, but indeed, had made some bad choices and was suffering the consequences of those choices. It only took a few sessions for Steve to start to see that what you *do* does not determine who you *are*; although he had made some bad choices, it did not make him a bad person. One of the most important things you can do is draw a line, a hard and fast line, right across the middle of the Self-Worth Pyramid that represents a hard barrier that will not to let any criticism about what you have done flow down and impact who you are. Imagine the power this will have in your life.

This lesson has strong personal significance to me. I learned something about self-worth as a teenager. Within six months after my mother abandoned us, my father remarried. It was a difficult time, as I went from a being in a family of four (my father, brother, sister, and me) to a family of nine. I went from being the middle child of three to the middle child of seven. Almost from the start my stepmother was unusually hard on me. I now understand that she was doing what she felt was best; but it was deeply painful to be berated and put down constantly. Now, on one hand my father would tell me that I could do anything I put my mind to; but on the other hand, I was getting the opposite message from my stepmother that I wasn't worthy of success, praise, or accomplishment. I lived with intense conflict.

As a teenager it became so bad that I began to question my self-worth and experienced compelling feelings of worthlessness. Nothing I did was good enough. My teenage world was crashing down on me. One night when I was feeling particularly lonely and worthless, I had a dream. In this dream my late grandfather came to me and said something that changed my life. He said, "If she only knew you. If she would only take the time to really get to know you, she would not treat you that way."

This was a turning point in my life. I realized then that my step-mother was only acting on what she knew, and all she knew was what I was *doing*. She had no clue as to *who* I was. She had not invested in getting to know *me*, who I was and what I was all about. I learned at this young age that there is a difference between *what we do* and *who we are*. Don't give people who criticize you the power to determine *who* you are, because if they really knew you, if they really took the time to get to know you, *I mean really know you*, they would see that you are a wonderful person, you are a great representation of God's creation, and you are worthy of respect, love and greatness. Don't let what you *do* determine who you *are*.

Low Self-Worth Creates a Vicious Cycle

Most people lump all of their self-worth and self-confidence issues into one bucket and come to the conclusion that they have low self-esteem. The question becomes, how do you know? How do you know if you have low self-esteem, low self-confidence or low self-worth? Having low self-worth and self-confidence is a lot like bad breath – it is much easier to detect in others than it is to detect in ourselves.

Low self-worth can be described as having a low opinion of your-self and feelings of being unworthy. The biggest problem with believing you have low self-worth is that you act according to that belief, and your actions then reinforce your belief, creating a vicious cycle that is difficult to break. It is usually in the midst of this cycle that a client will come to see me for help. Low self-worth is at the core of most of the problems that my clients want me to help them solve. The health of our self-worth affects every aspect of our life. From a job interview to an argument with your child or spouse, low self-worth causes seemingly small issues to become exaggerated and worse than they really are.

If you believe you are unworthy of love, you will act as though you are unworthy of love. If you believe you are an outcast, you will act as if you are an outcast. Your beliefs define your reality. In truth, you are so much more than what you believe about yourself. These beliefs, who you believe you are, when created from a position of low self-worth create what I call mistaken certainties. These mistaken certainties, invalid beliefs, about our self-worth will limit the joy and happiness we can feel. They will limit the fulfillment we could feel in our relationships and in most everything we do.

Steve came to me with what he considered a major problem. He was falling in love with a blond. At first I almost laughed, until he explained that every woman with blond hair whom he had dated had dumped him. He really loved this woman, but could not get past the fear that she, like the others, would surely dump him. You may think this ridiculous, but to Steve, it was as real as being afraid to see the dentist or being afraid of heights. He came to me insecure, unsure of what to do, and he felt certain that he was a failure with blonds. Steve was operating under a mistaken certainty. Although our nemesis may not be blond women, it is likely to be something else that we allow to minimize our self-worth, something false that we accept as truth.

Another example is someone who might say they are not good at math. What does it mean that someone is not good at math? Does it mean they are incapable of balancing their checkbook or that they can't remember how to calculate the area of a circle? Does it mean they can't figure out the price of something on sale at a 15% discount or that they can't convert gallons into liters? To make a statement of final judgment, like, "I am no good at math," is a mistaken certainty because it is an incorrect statement about *WHO YOU ARE,* rather than an accurate statement about what you can or cannot *DO.* There is a difference, and you need to be careful not to confuse the two and create a self-image based on mistaken certainties that limit your ability to be happy, to enjoy new experiences and to feel satisfied and content.

Over time this vicious cycle of low self-worth becomes quite powerful because it reinforces itself. Here is how it works. If you have a low opinion about yourself, it will create mistaken certainties, as I described above. You then act on that belief, and because it was a mistaken certainty, it produces unwanted results. In other words, it becomes a self-fulfilling prophecy. The unwanted results operate to reinforce your already-low opinion of yourself, and so the cycle continues. You don't have to live in this cycle any longer. The I AM STRONG formula will provide you with the skills needed to break this cycle and create a new cycle that reinforces a high opinion about yourself. And when that happens, you will reap all the benefits that I explained earlier.

Chapter 3

The Upside of Low Self-Worth

Motivational speakers and authors will tell you how bad it is to have low self-worth and low self-esteem. But if it is all that bad why do we put up with it? Could there be any upside to feeling worthless? You may think I am being sarcastic, when, in truth, I am asking an honest question. A state of helplessness and worthlessness can seem like a safe place to be because it justifies and allows you to protect yourself from the pain you might suffer if things go wrong or if you are rejected. For example, if you already know you are no good, it doesn't hurt as bad when no one will hire you or care enough to listen to you. If you already feel you are not worthy of being loved, you are validated when rejection comes your way, as it does for all of us; you knew it was going to happen anyway.

Feeling helpless gives you a false sense of safety because it seemingly excuses you from taking risks. People who feel worthless usually don't carry the burden of trying to succeed in anything that matters because they believe there's simply no point. Believing you probably won't succeed may seem like a safe place to be because you don't have to risk failure or rejection or accept more responsibility. If you act as if your opinions, thoughts and feelings are worthless, then people leave you alone and you are not asked to offer your opinion or participate. People who feel that they have no valuable skills or talents feel safe because no one will ask them to apply them. When you say you are useless, hopeless and a failure, then people lower their expectations of you, sometimes to the point of having no expectations at all. You can live a life free of the expectations of others. This can be your way of getting sympathy and attention, and you can sit back in your safe cocoon waiting for someone to come and rescue you from your worthlessness.

For some of you this may be all you know. Perhaps you have lived with feelings of inadequacy and unworthiness for so long that you don't know any better and you have come to think this is just the way you are. Feeling worthless, unworthy and helpless has become your normal. However, you are not your programming; you are not what others have said about you. You are so much more. It's time to create a new normal, a normal that is full of hope, full of power, and full of feelings of being worthy of success, love and fulfillment.

If you suffer from low self-worth and self-esteem, you also suffer from low self-confidence, all of which can have a negative effect on most aspects of your life. Here are some of the things that you will experience:

> Over-sensitivity – you are easily offended and feel that others are judging you

> Need/desire for praise

> Constant seeking of external validation

> Boasting and bragging to lift yourself up

> Judging others

> Feeling stupid, fat, ugly, useless, or unwanted

> A strong sense of never being good enough

> Not feeling strong enough to handle things on your own

> Feeling the need to be more articulate, prettier, smarter, richer, etc.

> Finding it hard to forgive yourself for making mistakes

> Dissatisfaction with life

- Depression

- Low energy levels

- Feeling helpless to change things

- Feeling either superior or inferior to others, never equal

- Withdrawing from social contact

- A sense of defeat and hopelessness

- Fear of social interaction

- Lack of care about the way you look, including poor hygiene

- Overall unhappiness

You are More than You Realize

Over the past few years I have learned to cook. I would not call myself a good cook, but I have learned to cook several of my favorite dishes and treats. Soft pretzels are my favorite and my family's favorite, as well. One of the key ingredients to making exceptional soft pretzels is yeast. As any of you who cook know, yeast must be activated in order for it to work. Yeast is activated with warm water. Your self-worth is like the yeast, always there waiting to be activated. Once your self-worth is activated, you are on your way to self-actualization.

You may or may not be familiar with the term self-actualization. It was originally introduced by theorist Kurt Goldstein in his book *The Organism: A Holistic Approach to Biology Derived from Pathological Data in Man.* Goldstein suggests that self-actualization is the motive to realize one's full potential. Abraham Maslow used the term somewhat later in his article *A Theory of Human Motivation,* where he defines self-actualization as "the desire for self-fulfillment." In fact, in Maslow's Hierarchy of needs that was proposed in the article, self-actualization is the highest of needs and can be obtained only after our other needs (physiological, safety, love/belonging, and esteem) are met.

I would like to borrow both definitions to describe a step in the process of growing and 'actualizing' your self-worth. Your self-worth - your sense of being worthy of happiness, reaching your potential, and being fulfilled and satisfied with all that life has to offer - should be at the very core of *who* you are. Whether you believe yourself to be a blessed child of a great and loving God or a natural being full of intelligence and wonder, actualizing your self-worth should be a motivating and guiding force in your life. It can become the source of alignment and flow to accomplish great things that once felt impossible. When you pursue any goal, when you dream any dream, when you wish any wish, it is a manifestation of your self-worth. If you are single and make the decision to date again, it is your self-worth and desire for self-actualization that will help propel you to that goal. If you want to climb Mount Fuji, it is your self-worth at your core that will provide the energy for all of the preparation that needs to take place in order for you to be successful. In this way it is the motive to realize one's potential. Self-actualization is also the culmination and outcome of the I AM STRONG formula, which will help you recognize and develop your sense of worth and derive your value from the inside, and not from external sources.

Look in the mirror. You can like what you see. You can appreciate all that you are, even with all of your flaws, idiosyncrasies and weaknesses. There are those around you who love you and want the very best for you. Don't ignore their love; discover what they see in you, the essence of you, and plant the seed of self-worth and let it grow within you. Look back on your past and, instead of seeing heartache and adversity, let the fact that you made it this far and have overcome so much become a core part of your self-worth. You can do hard things, you can overcome, and you can be triumphant. You can reach your potential - but only if your self-worth is healthy and strong. While you may be tempted to change your circumstances to find fulfillment, I recommend investing in your self-worth first, creating a worthy core of value, so that when you change your circumstances you don't end up repeating past mistakes.

Unlike self-esteem and self-confidence, self-worth is something we are born with. We were all born with high self-worth. As an infant and as a toddler we inherently knew we were valuable and worthy of our goals, dreams and wonder. It is only as we grow up and witness how the world responds that we allow our self-worth to be manipulated. High self-worth is not just a pipe dream or elusive concept; it can be your reality if you take it seriously and purposefully take steps to feel your inherent worth, to see yourself as worthy of success, happiness, and contentment.

For many years it was in vogue to talk about escaping to a distant, remote location to 'find yourself,' and I still hear that beckoning call from clients who feel they have lost their 'self' to being a wife, a mother, a father, a husband, an employee or some other cause. For many of you this is a real and serious situation. I have met many women, and men for that matter, who are lost to themselves. They look in the mirror and don't recognize who they have become. They feel alone, in conflict, and can't find their way back, and they can't find their way forward because they don't know where they are or where they're going. While I believe in giving service, giving of yourself to others and to good causes, I strongly believe there also needs to be a strong sense of self-care. When you give so much to others without eventually considering the cost of not taking care of yourself, you soon find yourself wondering who you are.

Service to others alone does not cause you to have this feeling of being lost. That happens when that service is not balanced with at least a moderate amount of self-care and protection of your self-worth. It also happens when you allow part of yourself to be broken, beaten down and criticized to the point of losing your own identity. I can recall just a few years ago when several of my friends were laid off and felt lost. They had become so identified with their job and career that when they lost their job, they lost their identity. Perhaps that describes you, that you have lost the identity of your true self to something else. No matter what it is, the effect is the same: you feel as if you don't know the person you are, and you long for the confident, capable, creative and wonderful person you thought you were.

That person is not gone for good; it is simply dormant and needs to be re-discovered and awakened. Once awakened, you will naturally recognize, feel and empower your true self-worth.

The next few chapters will guide you through the I AM STRONG formula to build your self-worth. Notice I did not say 'create' your self-worth. You don't need to create it, as much as you need to recognize it and build it up from where it is. You already have worth, you are already capable of so many things. You are strong!

Part 2

Putting the
I AM STRONG Formula
into Action

I AM STRONG!

"I looked in the mirror this morning and instead of seeing a cowardly 50-year-old with problems, I saw a capable and confident woman that could handle anything that comes my way. What a change a few weeks has made." This is what Heidi told me after four visits in 60 days. She had taken the I AM STRONG formula seriously and implemented the skills found in the next few chapters.

The formula is only as powerful as you allow it to be. You will find some of the skills easier to implement than others, but if you are serious about building your self-worth, esteem yourself highly, and becoming more confident, this formula will change your life. I understand that you may be skeptical, but in reality, you have nothing to lose. Have faith and trust in the process; I am confident that there are at least two or three things in these chapters that will make all the difference for you. Each part of the formula is followed by one or two practical tips. You may also want to pause here and take a few minutes to complete the self-worth assessment located at the end of Part 2 of this book to help you determine your current state of worthiness.

As a reminder, here are the elements of the I AM STRONG formula:

I is for Identify

A is for Acknowledge and Accept

M is for Minimize Your Weaknesses and Maximize Your Strengths

S is for Self-Recognition

T is for True to You

R is for Respect Your Needs

O is for Own It!

N is for Nourish

G is for Genuine

I AM STRONG!

Chapter 4

I is for Identify

Self-worth is a very real and powerful asset that can help you reach your dreams and re-discover your true value, potential and purpose. Increasing your self-worth begins with two essential steps. The first step is to recognize your self-worth for what it is and how it can be one of your greatest personal assets, which we have discussed. The next step is to understand and identify where and how you derive your value. I suggest you pause in your reading and spend a few minutes taking the Self-Worth Inventory and Assessment at the end of Part 2 of this book. Answering the questions will enable you to determine your current level of self-worth. Once you know your score, come back to this place in the book and continue reading, as I share with you a few practical and real-world indicators of your self-worth. As you learn about each of these indicators, try to resist the temptation to apply the indicators to others. Do your best to determine how these indicators show up in your own life.

Do you Derive your Value from Praise?

Emotional addictions are just as powerful and can be just as devastating as the physical and mental addictions that include nicotine, drugs and alcohol. One such emotional addiction is praise. We all want to be acknowledged and validated, but when our self-worth or our self-esteem depends on the praise of others, we may have a praise addiction. A praise addiction is a clear indicator that your self-worth could use a boost.

Praise addiction is characterized by a lifestyle that revolves around eliciting positive attention from others by putting yourself in situations where you strive for recognition or by surrounding yourself with friends who consistently flatter you, giving you the fix you so desperately need. Just like other addictions, you will feed the high associated with a fix, as well as the despair that comes as the high wears off. The ups and downs of praise addiction require serious consideration.

Praise, when given and received appropriately, is valuable feedback that helps us know we are on the right track. As parents we need to praise our children moderately, sincerely and effectively. For example, if Johnny did a good job, not a great job, of cleaning his room, the praise should be appropriate to a good job. Otherwise, if you over-praise him he is not likely to learn how to gauge his own actions well. He may grow up thinking that a good job is a great job. Nor is he likely to learn to validate himself instead of depending on your validation. Many parents over-praise or flatter their children in an attempt to raise self-esteem. Self-esteem grows from doing, accomplishing, achieving – not from praise. Confidence without competence is arrogance. It is quite possible that well-meaning parents, teachers and other mentors have conditioned you to only feel valued when you are praised. Don't fall into that trap! You are good enough, even if no one tells you that you are.

As with other addictions the first step to recovery is to recognize and then admit you have a problem. This is generally very difficult. Praise addicts can't just ask a friend because their friends are the most likely supply of this powerful drug. If you crave attention from others, if you consistently feel despair if someone hasn't said something nice or praised you in some way, then you are an addict.

My suggestion is to not quit 'cold turkey.' Recovery from praise addiction is similar to other addictions, in that it is an 'inside out' process. After recognizing you have a problem, I recommend that you start to substitute self-love principles in place of the praise you crave.

This requires some soul-searching and learning to see yourself as worthy, loveable, and sufficient. Remember, your default nature is divine; you have great qualities and you have great strengths. Be objective and honest with yourself and learn to savor your own accomplishments without needing or requiring others to flatter or praise you.

For many people the road to recovery includes a religious or spiritual component. This is also usually the case with recovery from other, often more recognized, addictions. Learning to rely upon a higher power (which, for me, is God) as your source of praise, your source of love, you can then use that love as a basis for recovery. You are divine; you have all you need to feel love and be loved. As you let God's love distill upon you, the need for praise from others is diminished.

Let me be clear, it's not the praise itself that is bad; it is the craving and need to support the addiction by a praise-lifestyle. You may not have severe praise addiction, or perhaps you only crave the praise and validation from a particular person. Nevertheless, you crave the praise because of low self-worth. Strengthening your self-worth by practicing the skills included in this section will help you love yourself, for who you are, even with all of your flaws and inadequacies.

Practical Tip:

Pay attention to how you feel when you are praised. Does it give you an emotional high? Contrast those feelings with how you feel when you are not praised, whether it's because you don't receive due recognition or because there has simply been a time lag since you were last praised. If either situation causes you to feel anxious, you may have a mild to strong case of praise addiction.

Identify your Inner Voice

Who is that voice inside your head? Of the thousands of conversations you have with yourself, how many are positive? The majority of the people I talk to admit that the conversations they have with themselves are mostly negative. This is particularly true for those of you suffering from depression and anxiety. Self-talk is a reflection of your self-worth and your self-esteem. If your self-talk is mostly negative, it reflects a wounded self-worth.

Imagine for a moment that I have a very special device. It is a small electronic device about the diameter of a bottle cap and as thin as a wafer. What makes this device special is that when placed just behind the ear, like a hearing aid, it will broadcast your thoughts so others can hear what you are thinking. If I were to place this device on you, how embarrassed would you be for everyone to hear what you are thinking? This question is most often met with tension and anxiety in my seminars. I would venture to guess that most people would be embarrassed, and it is shameful that you probably say worse things to yourself and about yourself than you would ever speak about another person. Of all the people in the world, of all the people whom you know personally, of all the people whom you would consider to be close friends, which person deserves to be spoken to tenderly and kindly? That person is you! I don't care if you are standing in front of the President of the United States or the Pope or your favorite celebrity, no one deserves your utmost respect more than you do. Each negative word, each negative phrase, each foul word you utter in your mind adds to your experience here on earth. Nothing you think is without an effect.

For some of you, your negative self-talk has become so commonplace that you hardly notice it anymore. The berating and barrage of slander is never-ending, and it has become the normal voice you hear every day, all day long. It is time to take notice of how you speak to yourself. Your thoughts create your world, not the other way around. James Allen, the eminent philosopher and psychologist, said, "Every impure and selfish thought you send out comes back to you in some form of suffering; every pure and unselfish thought returns to your in some form of blessedness."[2] This is even truer regarding your thoughts about yourself. William James, an early 19th century philosopher, said, "The greatest discovery of our age has been that we, by changing the inner aspects of our thinking, can change the outer aspects of our lives." Changing what we think and say to ourselves about ourselves will have a direct impact on our life's experience.

I have found that many of my clients are confused, thinking that their moods create their thoughts, and if they can just improve their mood or feel better, then their thoughts will follow suit. The opposite is actually true. You cannot have angry feelings or be in an angry mood without first having angry thoughts. "Every positive and negative feeling is a direct result of thought. It is impossible to have jealous feelings without first having jealous thoughts, to have sad feelings without first having sad thoughts, to feel angry without first having angry thoughts. It is impossible to feel depressed without having depressing thoughts," says author Richard Carlson.[3]

Your self-worth and your thoughts are interconnected. To improve your mood you need to improve your thoughts; and to improve your thoughts you need to first increase and improve the health of your self-worth. Low self-worth is characterized by negative, and often abusive, self-talk. I am not a fan of trying to control thoughts in order to improve your life. I am, however, a strong proponent of learning how to increase your feelings of self-worth so that your negative self-talk will begin to feel awkward and uncomfortable.

Practical Tip:

When you hear your inner voice say something negative, imagine a HUGE RED STOP SIGN in your mind to stop the negative thought; then replace the thought with a positive affirmation about yourself. The positive affirmation can be as simple as saying, "I refuse to disrespect myself that way," or "I AM STRONG and worthy of respect." Traditional affirmations may be quite helpful here as well. Once you place the huge red STOP sign in your mind, replace it with a HUGE GREEN SIGN that simply reads, "You are great!"

Practical Tip:

Another way to help you convert your negative self-talk to be more positive is to actually argue with yourself. When you notice that your self-talk is a self-criticism, respond by saying, "That's not true!" I recommend that you say it out loud for the greatest impact. This will help retrain your thought pattern to reflect your growing self-worth.

Identify your Comfort Zone

Another indicator of your self-worth is how you react to trying something new or finding yourself in a new situation. Your self-worth, self-esteem and self-confidence all come into play when you are asked try something new. Your reaction, both internally and externally, will largely depend on how much you fear rejection or failure. Your fear of rejection and failure has its foundation in self-worth. It is the level of fear we associate with failure and rejection that creates our comfort zone. While our level of comfort will greatly depend on the situation and our preparation, our reaction to trying new things, whether it is a new job, a new project, a new food, a new hobby, greatly depends on our self-worth. People with low self-worth tend to be risk–averse, while those with high self-worth tend be more comfortable with taking risks. This does not mean that, just because someone doesn't want to go skydiving, they have low self-worth. Nor does it mean that extreme risk-takers necessarily have high self-worth; I am sure we have all met people who have high self-confidence and take a lot of risks as a way of overcompensating for low self-worth. But being comfortable with taking a wise and appropriate risk is one self-worth indicator that has as strong self-confidence component.

Tanya was certainly not a woman whom I would characterize as shy and timid. I found her to be articulate, outgoing and sociable, and she appeared to be so well adjusted that I wasn't sure why she needed a life-coach. However, it didn't take long to understand that Tanya was suffering from an extremely restrictive comfort zone, to the point that her friends considered her neurotic. Tanya's fear of rejection and fear of new experiences had negatively impacted, and in some instances crippled, her social life, her home life, and her work. Recently her manager had asked her to take an assignment. It would be great a experience, look good on her resume and put her in good standing for a promotion. But she would have none of it and flatly told her manager, no. When I asked her why not, it took quite some time to get down to the real reason – she was afraid of failing. Once we got to the heart of the matter, Tanya made great progress and was able to take on the new assignment and did quite well. While she didn't get promoted by doing the assignment, the courage she found within herself to try new things was better than any promotion.

What is the internal conversation you have with yourself when you are about to try something challenging or something new? Are you able to list all the reasons why you shouldn't try, or do you experience anxiety just thinking about it? For many of you the fear of rejection and failure is very real and is likely based on past experience, when you were rejected or did not succeed at something important.

There is no guarantee that you will succeed at everything you try, and so anything new represents a risk. But it is also true that there is no guarantee that you will fail at everything, either; so it comes down to choice. Do you choose fear or do you risk succeeding?

Tanya hated to hear the word 'no.' To her 'no' meant rejection, and part of her anxiety of trying new things had to do with that fear of rejection, which she associated with her definition of 'no.' The first thing I worked on with Tanya is something that has worked for multiple clients and may work for you.

Practical Tip:

A simple exercise that I use with clients and in corporate settings is to get with a partner, where one person is to ask the other a series of questions. The questions don't matter; they can be anything at all. They can be yes/no questions or open-ended questions. Questions can be repeated. The other person is to answer every question with just one word, and that word is 'no.' Most of us have grown up to think that no is a negative response. While the word itself is a 'negative,' we don't have to interpret it as scary and intense, nor does it have to mean personal rejection. The goal is to ask and answer questions for five minutes without stalling or stopping.

When I used this practical tip with Tanya, she asked the questions and I answered with a 'no.' After about a minute she was bored with the exercise, as you might be, but I convinced her to continue. We repeated the exercise for several subsequent sessions with great success. The hard part is not answering but coming up with questions. The goal is to repeat this exercise until being told 'no' does not conjure up feelings of rejection. It is a simple exercise that, for some people, has remarkably profound results.

I AM STRONG!

Many times the fear of rejection or the fear of failure is much greater than the rejection or failure itself, and if you suffer from this fear there can be intense anticipatory anxiety. In other words you worry yourself sick over something that has not happened yet. Along with the 'no' exercise, I also helped Tanya learn another very important skill that is also quite simple and is often taught to people suffering from depression and anxiety. I helped Tanya learn to ask herself this simple question: "What is the worse that could happen?" Too often it is not that we can't deal with the rejection or the failure, it is that we just don't want to. Considering worst case scenarios will help you try to assess the potential outcome objectively. However, if you stop there, you may never reach actually overcoming your fear. The next question you MUST ask yourself is this, "What is the best that could happen?"

Too often we think in terms of extremes: black and white, right or wrong, all negative or all positive. It has been my experience, as I am sure it has been your experience as well, that most things end up neither as the worst that could happen, nor as the best that could happen. Outcomes or consequences of our choices typically fall somewhere in between. But either outcome is possible. If you decide the risks are worth it, you now have another choice: you can either focus on the worst possible outcome or the best. By learning to focus on the best possible outcome and almost forgetting the worst, you replace negative emotions (dread, emotional paralysis, etc.) with positive emotions (hope, excitement, etc.) and drastically reduce your fear of rejection or failure. These simple skills helped Tanya enormously, and I am sure they can help you too. Learning to risk rejection or failure is needed to overcome the fear of it.

We all feel different degrees of security and insecurity, based on our life experiences and present situations. I do not suggest that people with high self-worth have no insecurities. What I am suggesting is that as your self-worth grows, so do your self-esteem and your self-confidence to the point that you are able to take healthy risks and learn from them. This process enables you to become more confident in new situations and new experiences.

Practical Tip:

You can learn to stretch your comfort zone by:

> Engaging in low-risk activities that are new.

> Accepting that some situations may cause anxiety or nervousness, and that's ok.

> Starting with the easier tasks first, graduating to the harder things next.

> Choosing to be courageous.

> Creating a positive dialogue with yourself.

Practical Tip:

Anticipatory or anecdotal anxiety is often characterized by "what if" statements. If you find yourself experiencing anxiety with regard to future events, one way to help resolve the anxiety is to ask yourself these questions:

Is what I am thinking reasonable?

Is it realistic?

Is it rational?

The what-ifs you anticipate rarely happen because they are not rational, realistic or reasonable.

Identify Overcompensating

As an indicator of self-worth, self-esteem and self-confidence, overcompensating is difficult to assess. Just as I explained with the Self-Worth Pyramid, where self-worth is about who you are and self-confidence is about what you do, we tend to judge others, not based on who they are, but on what they do. Prominent author and speaker Charles Swindoll says, "Most of us have better sight than insight.

There is nothing wrong with our vision; it's perspective that throws us the curve. That is especially true when it comes to people. We tend to only see what we want to see, we see the obvious but overlook the significant. We focus on the surface while we fail to sense what is deep down inside."[4] For instance, we may think someone is a great person because they have a lot of self-confidence; and we think they have a lot of self-confidence because that is what we see. However, if we look a bit deeper, we may see that some people exaggerate their self-confidence in an effort to compensate for low self-worth. It is much easier to fake confidence than it is to fake self-worth. That said, the purpose of this particular illustration is not about judging others; but it's a helpful way to understand the principle so that you can apply it to yourself. It is about taking a good hard look at yourself and your actions to determine if you are focused on self-development from the perspective of what you do or from the perspective of who you want to become.

Not that long ago I started exercising regularly for the first time in my life. My goal was to become stronger and healthier than ever before in my life before my fortieth birthday. I achieved that goal mostly because I was using anger as a motivator to work hard and to be consistent with my exercise program. When the anger faded, my motivation plummeted. I had been overcompensating for feeling angry; when I dealt with the anger, I no longer had the same motivation. Fortunately, I was able to find a more positive form of motivation, rather than overcompensating. Remember that identifying overcompensating in ourselves is not so much about observing what we are doing, but why we are doing it. Other examples include the woman who feels she needs plastic surgery to be beautiful; someone who eats to compensate for feelings of worthlessness; the boss who uses intimidation and anger to compensate for feelings of self-doubt and inferiority. To some degree all of these individuals are overcompensating for low self-worth and would be far better off working on investing in their worth, rather than cosmetic surgery, food or bullying. Earlier in this section I discussed praise as an addiction. Some children overcompensate for a lack of praise or because they feel unloved by drawing attention to themselves through bad behavior, drugs, alcohol or pornography. In essence, their behavior is a cry for the love.

Overcompensation can take many forms. Anna feared not being valued by her manager and in staff meetings. This fear caused her to overcompensate by speaking loudly and being an emotional bully at work. Sam lacked confidence to speak up to his boss, so he overcompensated by bringing coffee to his boss every Friday to get on his 'good side.' While getting coffee for your boss is not wrong per se, it is the reasons behind it that should be examined. We all have a tendency to overcompensate. The goal is to recognize when we are trying to compensate for low self-worth and invest in creating a foundation of worth instead of perpetuating compensating behaviors.

Practical Tip:

Overcompensating can take many forms. The best way to determine if you are overcompensating is to begin to pay attention to why you do the things you do. For example:

» What do you most often do in your spare time and why?

» Do you try to mask emotional pain with drugs, alcohol or other destructive behavior?

» Do you exaggerate your own accomplishments, hoping to be noticed?

» Do you obsess over low-priority tasks?

» Watch for the reasons you engage in certain activities, and do them for the right reasons.

Identify your True Source of Value

Learning to identify where you derive your value is critical to this step in the I AM STRONG formula. However, once you identify your current sources, it is vital that you identify a true and reliable source of value or worth. As I mentioned above, external sources are inconsistent and unreliable. The only true source of your value is you! The next several steps in the I AM STRONG formula will help you reduce your reliance upon external sources and help you look to a powerful, reliable, and consistent source to determine your worth. You may want to assess your relationship to God or to a higher power. My higher power is God, so let me share with you what I mean from that context. God loves you; his love is unconditional and unchanging. There is nothing you can do to make God love you more, and there is nothing you can do to make God love you less. This is a powerful thing to consider because it demonstrates that you are worthy of his love regardless of what you do; he values you, cares for you, and is interested in your well-being unconditionally – because of who you *are*. The same is true for your higher power. This love can and should be the essence of your self-worth, even the very core. Why? Because it is unchanging, reliable and true.

If you are thinking that you are not worthy of that kind of love, that alone is an indicator that your self-worth is in need of repair. The additional steps in the I AM STRONG formula, along with the other parts of this book, will help you unload burdens from the past, forgive yourself, define your true purpose and help you experience joy and happiness. Even if you don't believe in God or feel you have a higher power, I encourage you to seek a true and reliable source of value that will grow within you as you continue to read and study the principles in this book. Remember, that in order to be a true and reliable source of your self-worth, it must come from within you and must not be dependent on anything external.

Self-Awareness

An important aspect of identifying where and how you derive your value is self-awareness. If you are like most people, you will likely answer that you 'feel' valued when you are sincerely appreciated or when you know you have made a significant contribution at work or to some other cause. Maybe you feel valued when you are complimented or validated in some way. While those things do make us feel good, self-worth, the value you place on yourself, is an inside job. To be truly effective and sustainable, your self-worth must be inherent, from the inside. Self-awareness is necessary step in understanding what motivates your actions, why you do what you do and how you ascertain your own value.

Katherine is one of the sweetest women you would ever meet. She is fun and outgoing and is the life of the party wherever she goes. However, Katherine is also very sensitive and would often get her feelings hurt by something someone says or does. When I asked her why those things hurt, her comment was, "Well, I don't know, they just do and when someone says something like that, it always hurts me; and I am tired of being hurt." Most of us get our feelings hurt sometimes, and often it is by the people closest to us. However, knowing you are hurt is only part of the equation. It is vitally important to become aware of why you are hurt, why it bothers and offends you. For example, through our coaching sessions I learned that Katherine was most often hurt when someone made her feel stupid. Feeling stupid was clearly a trigger emotion for Katherine. Once she became aware of it, we were able to focus on why that hurt her feelings and how increasing her own value, her self-worth, would make the biggest difference. This was not about what other people were saying to her, this was about how she derived her value.

Unfortunately, Katherine derived part of her value from having her intellect affirmed by others, especially people she held in high regard or authority. Together we uncovered that while growing up, her father insinuated that she was dumb; because of that she was hyper-sensitive to feeling stupid. We could have spent hours helping Katherine to learn to act and not react, to not believe it when others insinuated she was dumb; but that would have been like putting a band-aid on a knife wound. In a few short weeks of concentrating on helping her derive her value from within, to see herself as smart, capable, and wise, the comments or insinuations stopped bothering her as much.

> ## Practical Tip:
>
> Self-awareness requires you to become an observer. Just as you might people-watch at the mall, airport or grocery store, you now need to observe yourself. For now, don't get caught up in why you do certain things, just notice what you are doing.

What I call self-awareness others may call self-analysis. In this step I encourage you to take some time to understand who you have become and how you got to where you are right now. Using Garrett as an example, he was clueless as to how he got to a place in his life where no one wanted to spend time with him or interact with him. Within just a few sessions, Garrett was able to look at himself differently and, with some effort, realize that he needed to show interest in others in order to be seen as interesting. The same is true for you and me. Take some time to think about your reactions in certain situations, or about what offends you, how you deal with the happiness of others, or how well you take a compliment. Self-awareness is just that, becoming more aware of your 'self' so that you can start to make an honest assessment of your current level of self-worth.

Another aspect of self-awareness is being honest about your dependencies. Are you dependent upon someone else or something else in order to feel valued and appreciated? Do you seek situations where you can be a physical or emotional care-giver because that's where you derive your value? Are you emotionally co-dependent and feel happiness or contentment only when the person you are closest to feels happy? These are all indicators of the health of your self-worth. The majority of the people I speak to have the idea that self-worth is just something that happens over time and is a result of how much success or failure you experience in life. They believe it only natural that someone who has had many failures would have low-self worth and someone who has experienced a lot of success or pleasure would naturally have a high self-worth. Neither is true. Your circumstances do not determine your self-worth. Sure, if you consistently fail at something you may not have the same self-confidence as someone who does not fail, but it should not affect your self-worth.

The most important aspect of self-awareness is to truly know where and how you derive value. What makes you feel worthy of greatness? What makes you feel unworthy? Take some time to observe and analyze when you feel the most worthy and when you feel the least. These will be good indicators as to how much work you need to put into the next step, which is to establish a baseline of self-worth for yourself. Pay particular attention to whether your value is derived inherently, from the inside, or extrinsically, from outside sources. The more inherent your source of worth, the more powerful it will be. Self-awareness is about something deeper than just what you feel and when. I want you to dig deep, to look inside yourself and try to understand not only what makes you feel valuable but also why you feel valuable and where that value comes from. The goal will be to finally get to the point of realizing, truly feeling and experiencing, that you are inherently worthy of greatness, happiness and satisfaction no matter what happens to you. You are worthy just because you are you!

Practical Tip:

Self-awareness is best achieved by first becoming an observer of yourself (see the previous Practical Tip) and then trying to understand why. Following are a few questions to help you become more aware. Answer them without judgment – you are only observing.

- When you are with a friend or colleague ask yourself:
  - Why do I like spending time with them?
  - Who is doing most of the talking?
  - What am I feeling or thinking?
- While you are doing something fun ask:
  - Why do I like this?
  - What am I feeling or thinking?
- At random times during the day ask:
  - Where am I emotionally?
  - Why do I feel the way I do?

Chapter 5

A is for Acknowledge and Accept

Self-Acknowledgement

Once you become more self-aware, the next step is to acknowledge who you are. Many people confuse acknowledging something and someone as acceptance. For example, you may indeed acknowledge that you are not at your best in the morning. In fact, you may even refer to yourself as not being a 'morning' person. Yet, if you beat yourself up about being tired in the morning, you have only acknowledged it but have not accepted it. The same is true when it comes to our own character traits, quirks and idiosyncrasies. We may acknowledge them but have yet to accept them. You cannot change what you are unable to acknowledge.

Let me give you an example. Allison had a problem with her husband that, in her mind, had become a deal-breaker. Her husband, Curtis, was lazy. His laziness was chronic and complete. He had a full-time job and was well respected by his supervisors and co-workers and didn't appear to be lazy at work. But at home he left his dirty dishes, dirty socks, old clothes, and unfinished projects lying around the house. After vacation Curtis would take weeks to unpack, leaving open suitcases on the floor of their bedroom. Allison was not what I would consider a neat-freak but definitely had a hard time with clutter.

Paul was in full denial about being lazy. There was something about the word itself that offended him, and week after week Paul denied being lazy. He provided elaborate justifications for leaving things lying around. He was aware of his behavior, Allison made sure of it; he even accepted that he did, at times, leave things lying around. What Paul lacked was acknowledging that he was lazy. Paul, like most of us, had a hard time seeing himself as lazy and felt that acknowledging it would be admitting defeat or failure. That is not what it means. Acknowledging something, a character flaw or trait, a weakness, or something you need to improve, does not make you a failure at all. It is simply getting past denial and justification in order to be able to improve yourself. Again, we cannot change what we don't acknowledge.

How does this relate to self-worth? Becoming self-aware is a willingness to objectively consider if you need to work on your self-worth using the indicators mentioned in this section. Acknowledgement allows you to admit that you could use some help or improvement. It does not mean you are a failure. Acceptance of what you've become aware of about yourself and frankly acknowledged is the first step to changing for the better. Changing for the better yields joy and higher self-worth.

Acknowledgement breaks the vicious cycle of low self-worth at the belief level and allows you to replace negative beliefs about yourself with truly positive beliefs that will enable you to grow your self-worth. A word of caution – acknowledgment should not come with any self-indictment or judgment. Self-indictment, putting yourself down, and berating yourself was covered earlier in the discussion about negative self-talk. I will give you an example from my own life. In my 30s I loved to play basketball and often tried to join a pick-up game at the local YMCA. My love for the game was greater than my ability to play it well. I soon found that I was spending more time on the sidelines than playing in the game. When I finally asked a good friend what was going on, he confided in me that I really wasn't that good. He brought it to my awareness, and I denied it, thinking that I was being black-balled at the YMCA. But eventually I was able to admit that I wasn't as good as I thought I was. Once I finally acknowledged and accepted it, I was able to change my belief about my ability, which led to a behavioral change. I continued to play basketball, but instead of seething on the sidelines, I was grateful to get minutes in each game and enjoyed the whole experience much more.

Acknowledgment helps you see where you are on the journey to increasing your self-worth and helps you benefit most from the I AM STRONG formula.

Practical Tip:

Acknowledgement is actually self-admission without self-indictment. Here is how you can practice self-acknowledgement:

) Admit that you are not perfect and feel ok about it.

) Admit that you are unable to meet everyone's expectations.

) Admit that there may be a tiny bit of truth to what others say about you, and that it is ok.

) Admit that you have some weaknesses, but they don't define you.

) Admit that though you could be better, you are wonderful, capable, smart and beautiful.

) Admit that you are inherently worthy of greatness!

Self-Acceptance

There is nothing wrong with dreaming and intending to be better, to be more, and to be great. All of that is good and can help you cope with present circumstances, just as it is important to recognize that you are not your job, you are not your body, you are not a disease, a situation, nor are you a role, such as a widow, a divorcee, a mother, etc. Dreaming, wishing, intending and wanting more is great when it starts from a strong foundation of self-worth. Self-acceptance helps you create that foundation by accepting who you are in right this moment without self-indictment, self-judgment or denial. Self-acceptance is a powerful concept that will allow you to reach greatness. Acceptance is not giving up, giving in or settling for less. Acceptance does not mean you stop dreaming, wanting or desiring more, it means you are going to be objective about who you are and where you are starting from.

"… ye shall know the truth, and the truth shall make you free."[5] Students of The Bible often think of this verse as referring to religious truth, but I like to think that it has a greater application in our own lives as it refers to the 'truth about ourselves.' Knowing the truth about ourselves does indeed set us free. You cannot fully participate in self-acceptance without knowing the truth, yet many of us live in denial, rather than being truthful with ourselves about who we are. This has been true in my own life. For many years my wife would refer to me as an 'angry man.' Never had I thought of myself as an angry man. I found it particularly hard to even picture myself as an angry man, let alone believe it to be true. Passionate, sure. Angry? No! Years went by, and I remained in denial that I was an angry man. As long as I was in denial, I was not in acceptance and was, therefore, unwilling to address what my wife was recognizing as an obstacle to our shared happiness. As soon as I accepted it, first as *her* truth, then as *a* truth about myself, I was able to address it and conquer it.

It was a difficult thing to do. But once I became self-aware, acknowledged the truth about myself and accepted it, I was no longer in denial and could objectively address it. The truth set me free from denial and from having to remain an angry man. This was not 'giving in,' nor was this in any way 'admitting defeat.' This was becoming willing to consider feedback about myself as being true, acknowledging the truth in it, and then accepting it. The acceptance allowed me to work on it, to see it for what it was and to realize that there were indeed times when I was angry but didn't realize it. Without the acceptance there could have been no progress.

I recently had a couple come to me for coaching. I will refer to this couple as Jack and Jill. Jack and Jill were at the point of separating because of what Jill called 'extreme control issues.' Every time the word 'control' even came up in the session I could see Jack cringe, and his body language reflected total and complete denial. Jill complained that Jack insisted that they go to bed at the same time and that, once in bed, Jill could not leave. He also insisted that she telephone him whenever she left the house to tell him where she was going. She commented on his demanding sexual behavior and how he would get angry when she was unable or unwilling to engage in sexual intercourse every day. Jack and Jill had been high school sweethearts, and after 25 years of marriage, Jill was demanding that Jack change, that he learn to be less controlling, or she would leave.

In session after session Jack would argue that he was not controlling and would attempt to justify and rationalize his actions. As long as Jack was unwilling to accept Jill's comments as *her* truth and then accept it as *a* truth about himself, there was no progress to be made. A breakthrough finally came when I asked Jack what would be so wrong with accepting that he is controlling. There are certainly worse traits to have. This was hard for Jack, as it might be for you to accept something about yourself that is so contrary to the image you have about yourself. This is why 360-degree feedback exercises in the workplace are so effective because it challenges your self-image and forces you to see yourself as others see you. Granted, the feedback or perception of others is not always 100% accurate, but you would do yourself a world of good to not dismiss it outright.

Self-acceptance is an important element of self-worth, as it allows you to see yourself for who you are with all of your talents, strengths, greatness, flaws, weaknesses and quirks. A critical part of acceptance means shedding self-expectations and the expectations others have of you. Think of it this way: self-acceptance is akin to entering your starting location into a GPS system. It is simply an acknowledgement of your current location, situation and psyche. It is your starting point, not your end point. Remember, it is acceptance without self-judgment, self-indictment or self-condemnation. Following the GPS analogy, when you enter your starting location, it isn't about how you got there or why it might have been a good or bad decision that got you there; it is a simple acknowledgement of where you are. You are who you are; it is what it is. Get out of the should-haves, could-haves and what-ifs to recognize who, what and where you are without condemning the journey of how you got there. To awaken and rediscover your true value and inherent worth, an honest and objective assessment of your life is required.

Practical Tip:

Here are some questions you can ask yourself to help approach self-acceptance:

- What do I do that irritates others?
- What would someone say is my greatest weakness?
- How do you react to criticism and negativity? Why?
- When am I most offended?
- What is the one thing that someone could say to me that would hurt me the most?
- What motivates you?
- Are you dependent on anything, anyone, or any situation for your happiness?
- What threatens you?
- What builds you up?
- When do you feel happiest?
- When are you the most self-conscious?

What is most important in this exercise is that you start to see yourself as others do and accept the answers without judgment. To get a more complete picture of who you are, you could have a few people you know answer these questions about you as well.

Start paying attention to how you feel in certain situations and try to assess why you feel that way. Accept who you are as a starting point. Without an accurate idea of where you are starting from, you may not get to where you want to go.

Chapter 6

M is for
Minimize your Weaknesses
and Maximize your Strengths

Minimize your Weaknesses

You are not your primary flaw. Have you ever met anyone that has never made a mistake? You may know someone that can't admit it, but I mean someone who is perfect? No? Then you are in good company because we all make mistakes! It is possible that some of your mistakes have made a real mess of things. Perhaps you cheated on your husband. Maybe you have a DUI on your record.

Maybe it isn't your mistakes that bring you down. Maybe when you look at yourself in the mirror you see flaws instead of flowers, and each time you even think a single positive thought about yourself, you are quick to remind yourself just how bad you are. Naming your strengths is very hard for some of you. The easier question for some is to name your biggest flaw. Go ahead, what is it? Are you lazy? Do you cheat on every diet you have tried? Do you drink too much? Do you stay up to late? Do you blame yourself for every failed relationship? Whatever you consider to be your primary flaw, it does not define you!

You are not your problems, your situation, you checkbook or

your credit score. These things do not define you. Remember that self-worth is about who you are, not about what you do. So after I ask you to identify your primary flaw and you give me your answer, my response is, "So what!" When you over-generalize and characterize yourself according to one primary flaw, you do yourself a huge (and I do mean *huge*) disservice. I have heard so many people over the years say things like, "I can't seem to get going in the morning – I am just not a morning person," or "I can't go back to school; I am just too lazy." So what if you have a hard time getting going in the morning? I'll bet that if you won an all-expense-paid trip to Italy that required you to get up early in the morning to catch the flight, you wouldn't turn it down, saying, "Thanks, but I'm just not a morning person." Sure it might be hard, but you are not your primary flaw!

I want to counsel you also to not define yourself by a combination of smaller flaws and character traits. These smaller flaws, characteristics, quirks and traits are bothersome because we are constantly aware of them. They are easy to detect because we become quite sensitive to being reminded of them. These reminders from others can be a subtle raise of an eyebrow, a laugh at the wrong time, or when someone contradicts us. Don't get caught majoring in minor things! Let these things roll off your back, and don't lump them together into one big issue that causes you pain, embarrassment or regret.

Why not turn things around and define yourself by your greatest strength or talent? What is that? Take a minute to really consider what your greatest strength is, the one thing that someone would say about you if I asked them about you. Instead of self-deprecation, why not practice self-appreciation? I was once forwarded an email in which a friend was recommending me for a job. I am not sure it was meant for my eyes, but I was both flattered and embarrassed reading the very nice and generous things my friend was saying about me. One thing in particular has stayed with me. He said, "You can count on Kirk to do what he says he will do." I hadn't considered it before, but one of my strengths is that I am dependable. That is one of the strengths I now use to help value myself and to define who I am. What do you use? Are you loyal, dependable, strong, creative, friendly, helpful, sincere, fun...? That is what you should focus on. Don't let the part of you that you dislike become all of you! Don't suppose that your one major flaw is who you are. You are so much more. There is so much more to you than your flaws.

Maximize your Strengths

How well do you know and can you articulate your strengths? I realize that in a job interview you might answer with the strengths you believe will demonstrate why you are the best candidate for the job and may not necessarily be what, in all honesty, you would consider your greatest strengths. But I would like you will take some time to be honest with yourself and sincerely ponder this: what are your strengths? The question is meant for real, honest, and authentic soul searching. How well do you know what your gifts and your top strengths are?

Not that long ago, Julie came to my office for her first coaching session. I could tell she was a bit nervous and had obviously taken time to prepare for the session. She was dressed nicely in a fashionable skirt and blouse, her hair was freshly done, and her makeup was expertly applied. She sat with her arms folded. Although she wanted to be there, her posture and body language made her look as if she had just been sentenced to go to the principal's office. Our session started with me asking the questions and Julia giving one-syllable answers, such as "yes," "no," or "I don't know." I started to get anxious that Julia was certainly not getting her money's worth, so I changed directions. "Julia," I said, "Tell me what you like best about yourself?" Well, this question was also followed with, "I don't know. I am not sure how to answer that." After a long pause, I asked Julia who her best friend was. She replied, "Cathy." I then said, "If I were to ask Cathy about you, about what you do best, what your gifts are, what talents you have, what she would consider your greatest strengths, what would she say?"

The Julia that started speaking was completely different than the Julia who was sitting in my office a moment prior. From the perspective of Cathy, Julia described herself as talented, gifted, strong and secure. She seemed an amazing person to me, yet very different from the Julia who first entered my office. As our session continued, I realized that Julia had an intellectual understanding of her talents and strengths but did not BELIEVE that she was talented and strong; and that was the problem. Using her friend's perspective, we were able to engage in building Julia's belief in herself and in her capabilities with a tremendously positive result.

Could this be you? Could it be that intellectually you are aware of your strengths and that you may be surrounded by friends, family and others who truly see you as gifted and talented, but you don't believe it? Recognizing your strengths, talents, abilities, and unique gifts is an important part of the I AM STRONG formula. It will help you receive the strength to do hard things and feel worthy of great miracles and blessings. Recognizing and acknowledging your strengths and using them will bolster your self-worth and maximize its benefits. You will be able to handle stress, drama and adversity better. You literally become stronger by focusing on your strengths, rather than on your weaknesses.

It is time to stop minimizing the positive feedback you get from others, give yourself more credit and recognize your strengths. Here is an exercise to help you do this quickly: in less than one minute, name 5 to 10 of your strengths without hesitating or pausing. You may have to do this over and over again until you are able to name 10, but stick to it. There is a great learning that will take place as you do this exercise. You will train your mind to believe what others see in you; you will reduce your unbelief and grow your self-worth.

I AM STRONG!

Practical Tip:

Minimizing weaknesses and maximizing strengths go hand in hand. Here are some things you can do to put this into action:

- Create self-development time. Set aside 30 minutes a week to consider your strengths and choose what weakness you will work on improving over the following week.

- Surrender your weakness to God or your higher power.

- Begin to redefine yourself based on your strengths. Ignore any self-talk that accentuates your weaknesses.

- Ask five close friends to share with you what they see as your strengths and talents.

- Take a strengths assessment, such as StrengthsFinder or DiSC® assessment.

- Believe that you are STRONG!

I AM STRONG!

Chapter 7:

S is for Self-Recognition

Jerri had a hard time recognizing her needs. When asked what her needs were, she didn't even have the words to describe them. However, what alarmed me more was that, in order for Jerri to feel good about herself, she was dependent on the compliments and validation from others. Jerri is not alone in this. I imagine that there are many of you who also rely upon the validation from those around you to justify feeling that you are worthy and capable. This dependence on validation from external sources means your sense of worthiness is conditional, when your true self-worth really is and should be unconditional and independent of what others think or judge.

External sources of validation are fickle. The praise and validation we receive from others can be empty, insincere, conditional and inconsistent. I have had many clients whose need for external validation is so strong that when the external validation is absent, they fill the void with overeating, pornography, addictions and other destructive behavior. It is time to start looking at yourself in the best possible light. I realize that this may be hard because we have been trained to think that self-praise and self-recognition are evil and lead to such social transgressions as arrogance and boasting. Get over it! As long as you are objective and able to see yourself for all of who you are, there is nothing wrong with self-recognition.

Self-recognition is hard because we almost know too much about ourselves and the situations we commonly find ourselves in. We know our own intentions, as well as our outcomes. Sometimes our intentions are what keep us from true self-recognition. For example, let's say that we feed the poor and needy at a local soup kitchen but do it for the wrong reasons. Only we know of our intentions, which may actually be more selfish than concerned about those we are helping to feed. The truth about our attitude will be hard to swallow because we may not want to admit to ourselves the truth behind our actions; we may try to deceive ourselves and others about our intentions, making it difficult to see ourselves objectively as we really are. In contrast, self-recognition flows naturally if our actions align with our thoughts and our beliefs, or in other words, when we exercise integrity. Living with integrity is an important aspect of self-worth that is discussed in the next step of the I AM STRONG formula – T is for True to You. Otherwise, our own self-recognition is as empty as the insincere compliments we get from others.

I am in no way saying that all compliments are insincere or that we should refrain from giving and receiving compliments. In fact, giving and receiving sincere praise and compliments are important means of expressing love, as well as indicators of self-worth as mentioned previously. Receiving positive feedback is a valuable aspect of self-confidence and self-esteem, and listening to praise, as well as the filtered criticism of others, can help you improve your choices. What I want to do is raise your awareness of your dependence upon compliments and praise from others. We do not want to use external validation and praise as a means of deriving your self-worth. As I have mentioned several times, it merits repeating: self-worth comes from the inside.

Self-recognition is the ability to see and accept your goodness and recognize that you are worthy of greatness. Sure, when this is taken to the extreme it can lead to pride and conceit; but if done with balance and honesty, it can help you see yourself for the wonderful person you are without needing to hear or feel it from others. One way to practice appropriate self-recognition is to spend some quiet time contemplating being a child of God or a great creation of your higher power. Think on your relationship to God or your higher power; ponder deeply that you are loved and capable of love. From this you will feel the inner strength that comes from knowing you are inherently worthy of all that God has to offer.

Practical Tip:

Many of my clients have found that a daily practice of meditation to calm their body and their mind helps them feel God's love or the love from their higher power, which enables them to feel worthy of greatness and happiness.

When you come to see yourself as a strong, capable, beautiful, precious human being, you are able to put your weaknesses into their proper perspective and maximize your strengths. Not that long ago, I heard the story of a woman who had a stroke and struggled to walk without a walker or a cane. She felt she was physically strong enough, yet she wasn't able to take more than a step or two without needing support. She saw specialist after specialist, with no improvement. She was at the end of her wits when she told her family doctor she wanted to learn to walk without assistance. He asked her to stand up and take as many steps as she could. She stood and only accomplished a few. He then gave her great advice that we should all follow: he said, "You are putting too much weight on your weak side; shift your weight to your strong side, and you should be able to walk just fine." She did just that, and with very little practice, she became able to walk without a walker. As we do the same, minimize our weaknesses, not ignore them, but minimize them, and maximize our strengths, we too will be able to do hard things and receive the happiness and fulfillment we long for.

If you think about the people you like the most, the people you enjoy spending time with, you will notice that they are the people who tend to downplay your weaknesses and appreciate your strengths. You can do the same for yourself through appropriate self-recognition. The goal of self-recognition is to sever whatever dependence you have on validation or recognition from external sources. As mentioned above, those sources are inconsistent, unpredictable and can be insincere. True self-worth is recognizing yourself for your own greatness, believing you can do hard things and face whatever adversity life has to throw at you. This doesn't mean that you will go out seeking new adversity; rather, it means that you know and believe that you will be ok when it comes. You have a quiet inner confidence that it will all work out.

Practical Tip:

Here are a few tips to help you break free of the need for validation from external sources:

) Ponder and meditate your inherent worth – how marvelous you really are.

) Be quick to celebrate any achievement – especially the small ones.

) Remember that your own opinion matters more than what others think.

) Write in a journal and be purposeful about documenting your growth.

) Savor your previous accomplishments to recognize you are great! You are strong!

Chapter 8

T is for True to You

Low self-worth is not only something we have learned, it is also a result of not being true to ourselves. Think of someone you trust implicitly and why you trust them. Chances are they have gained your trust by being worthy of your trust; by their consistent reliability and honesty, they demonstrate that they are trustworthy. Trust is generally earned through the making and keeping of promises, such as when someone keeps their word by doing what they say they will do. Their talk and their walk are aligned. Self-alignment is critical to your self-worth. The greatest benefit from self-alignment is that you will be able to rise above the brute force of life and let the positive energy of the universe or the power of God, propel you along your desired path. Positive self-worth has energy, energy that can be harnessed and multiplied. Feeling inherently worthy allows you to rise above thoughts of deserving recognition or valuing yourself based on your achievements or possessions. A healthy self-worth allows you to relax into life and feel that you are worth greatness. When you align your beliefs, thoughts and actions with your values and desires, magic happens! Life suddenly becomes easier. Things you need seem to come to you spontaneously. Some authors and scientists have called this *flow*.

Referring to the Self-Worth Pyramid, we will add three very important qualifiers: beliefs, thoughts and behavior. This is where alignment needs to take place. As your self-worth becomes healthier,

Behavior ↔ Thoughts ↔ Beliefs

your beliefs about yourself change and become more positive. This should transform your thoughts about yourself or, in other words, increase your self-esteem. Your improved self-esteem will give you more confidence to accomplish your desires, duties and responsibilities. To demonstrate this principle of aligning beliefs, thoughts and behavior, let's say that you want to run a marathon (something you *do*) but *think* you may not be able to. This creates a conflict between your *behavior* (what you want to accomplish) and what you *think* about yourself. This conflict will diminish the energy you have to persevere through the training you need to complete the marathon. Now imagine that you truly believe that you can run the race; your thoughts become aligned with your belief, which now aligns with your desire. This alignment generates within you more energy to train and run the marathon. The energy created through aligning your beliefs, thoughts and behavior is available to you on any level for anything you want to accomplish. When this alignment does not occur, it creates conflict that can destroy your chances to complete the race.

Alignment is also apparent in our relationships with others. For example, if you don't think you are worthy of love (belief), yet you want to love and be in love (behavior), there is conflict that will diminish the love you feel and the love you are able to give. If you think you can do something but deep inside don't believe it, chances are you won't succeed either. Alignment in its most basic form means that you will walk the talk. This is why living a lie is so emotionally damaging – your behavior is in direct conflict with what you think and what you believe. This conflict will destroy your self-worth and your self-esteem and eventually cause you to misbehave or behave in ways that won't bring you your desired results.

A key component to alignment is integrity. As you keep your promises and are honest in your dealings with others, you become true to yourself and, in turn, make huge investments in your self-worth. As your self-worth grows, so will your self-esteem and self-confidence. Your trust and confidence in yourself, your intuition, your judgment and your opinions grows as well. You become worthy of your own trust, which is another form of being true to yourself. Imagine going into any situation, any relationship, any meeting, or any phone call with absolutely nothing to hide. Wouldn't you be the most confident you have ever been? The more you do this, the more trust you have that you will do the right thing for the right reasons. You will no longer second-guess yourself. As you trust yourself more and more, you will be able to trust others more, as well. That is what alignment can do for you. Aligning your beliefs, which include your values, with your thoughts and your actions frees you from lies, guile, manipulation, subterfuge, conspiracies and backbiting. You become true and free from emotional disguises and their accompanying stress and guilt. You are free to be who you are.

Another aspect of being true to yourself is doing the right thing for the right reason. This is often not as simple as it sounds when we have to do something we don't want to do or feel obligated to do. When we do the right thing for the wrong reason, we short-change ourselves and others. Patrick became very nervous in my office when I asked his wife, Valerie, to share a list of things he could do to show his gratitude and love for her. When asked why he felt nervous he said, "Once I know what is on her list, I will feel obligated. I will do it because I am forced to." Don't we all feel that way at one time or another? How can we be true to ourselves when we feel obligated to do something, whether or not we want to do it? Do we do it anyway, even if it is not for the right reasons? It is my experience that when this happens, the result is resentment. The way to stay true to yourself is to find a reason to do the right thing that is not in conflict with how you feel or what you value.

Patrick knew that showing gratitude and love for his wife in ways that made her feel loved was the right thing to do. Patrick's 'wrong reason' was *because he had to complete a checklist*. After some exploration, Patrick arrived at his 'right reason': because he loved Valerie. Tapping into those feelings of love for his wife motivated him to seek better understanding of his wife's needs. Once he understood what she was really saying, he realized he needed to categorize the things on Valerie's list, rather than look at the exact items as a specific to-do list that had to be checked off. For example, one thing on Valerie's list was that she wanted Patrick to pump gas for her. Initially, he thought she meant that they would go to the gas station together, and while she watched from the car, he would get out and pump gas. But that wasn't it at all. She wanted him to notice when she was busy and do a simple favor of filling up the gas tank of her car so she wouldn't have to.

Once Patrick understood the real meaning behind her list, he could think of several ways on his own to recognize Valerie's busy schedule and do small kindnesses for her. Rather than resenting her for not pumping her own gas, Patrick chose to understand the real meaning of her request, honor his wife's need to feel loved, and honor himself by aligning his love for her with her need for a little thoughtful help. In this way, he was able to remain true to himself. We can all do the same thing. When asked to do something you don't want to do, take the higher ground, look for the real meaning behind the request, and do the task with the right reason in mind. Granted, you may have to look hard for your 'right reason,' but it will be worth it to stay in alignment and to be true to yourself while honoring your responsibility to others.

What is Your True Identity?

What is your true identity? Do you identify yourself by who you are or by what you have done? Is your identity formulated by your job, a sport, your role as mother, father, breadwinner or caretaker? Perhaps your identity comes from what you consider your primary flaw or is strongly influenced by negative experiences in the past? Marisa had been divorced for more than four years. Her husband was abusive and manipulative to the point that Marisa felt damaged and unworthy of loving and being loved. Her identity was primarily based on what had happened to her. She identified herself as having been abused. She saw herself as a divorcee. But Marisa is more than a marital status. She is so much more than her pain, suffering and what happened to her in the past.

You are not your primary flaw. You are not your negative past. And yet, we all define ourselves to some degree by what has happened to us. A woman may define herself as a divorcee or as an abused child. Or you may consider yourself an 'old-maid' because you have not been married yet. Perhaps you were the star quarterback in high school and you long for the glory days, or at least for the same sense of accomplishment. Maybe you have made some big mistakes that continue to haunt you. Your past is something that makes you unique, special and a survivor, if not also a winner. Take a few minutes to look back on your life and consider your tragedies, your adversity, and your tough moments. Now consider how far you have come. Your true identity is more about who you are than what you have done. Defining yourself solely according to what has happened to you is being less than true to yourself. You are selling yourself short. Your true identity is so much more; it is based in how great you are, how marvelous and unique you are. In a later section you will learn how to turn your adversity into your advantage; but for now, don't let your negative past events determine your value. Obviously, you are greater than your past, or you would not be reading this book at this very moment. Have things turned out the way you planned? Probably not; but no matter how things have turned out, you have a choice to become better or to become bitter.

Practical Tip:

Practice aligning your beliefs, thoughts and behavior:

❭ Make and keep promises: even keeping a promise to be where you say you will be when you say you will be there is a good way to practice being true to yourself.

❭ Observe the internal conflict you experience when your actions are inconsistent with your core beliefs and values.

❭ Trust your decisions by sticking to them. Try not to second-guess your decisions.

❭ Recognize resentment as misalignment, and try to find the higher meaning in what you are asked to do.

❭ Do the right thing for the right reason.

Chapter 9

R is for Respect Your Needs

Let me once again use Jerri as an example. Jerri was mild mannered and appeared to be a kind, loving and generous person. She volunteered, baked bread for new neighbors, and was the greeter for Sunday services at her church. She prided herself in doing crafts and helping anyone in need. She was a dedicated mother and wife and seemed to be in good health. As we talked I began to notice that when she smiled (she smiled a lot), it was forced; and her laugh (she laughed a lot) was more of a nervous laugh than a hearty or wholesome, real laugh. From the outside Jerri seemed like she had it together, but I could tell that something was boiling on the inside. Without help she would eventually explode or, more likely, emotionally implode.

Jerri was quite talkative about mundane activities and events but said very little about herself and how she felt. When I asked how she felt about someone or something, her answers were, "I don't know how I feel about that," or "I will have to think about that." Then I asked the big questions. "Jerri," I asked, "what are your top needs?" After a very long pause (so long that I thought perhaps she had not heard the question), Jerri's response was the same as before, "I don't know." I continued to probe with questions like, "What makes you happy," and "When do you feel most at peace?" "What brings you the greatest joy?" All of the questions got the same response, until finally Jerri said to me, "Well, I do like it when people compliment me."

How many of you are like Jerri, so in tune with the needs, happiness, and fulfillment of others, that when asked, you have a hard time identifying and expressing your own needs? If you can't even express your needs, how can you stick up for them when challenged? Being self-assertive is not only becoming aware of your own needs but also growing in your ability to stand up for them and cherish them. This does not mean that you will only think of yourself, but rather, you will balance your needs with the needs of those around you so that you can invest in yourself while serving others. Service is a great aspect of being happy and making a contribution to others. However, you cannot give away what you do not have. If you are being charitable with others, yet do not show charity for yourself, what you give is minimized. In Jerri's case, she was oblivious to her own needs. Jerri needed some help in recognizing her needs, expressing them and sticking up for them.

It is important to note that Jerri's main issue was neither about her needs nor about being assertive, but had roots in low self-worth that was demonstrated in feeling that she was not worthy of the fulfillment of her own needs. How many of you find yourself in a similar situation, where you have needs but are unable to express them because you don't feel you are worth the effort? Perhaps you have allowed yourself to be trained to subordinate your feelings to the point of ignoring them. Well, guess what? You really can't ignore them because they will creep up in other aspects of your life. A quite common manifestation of this is resentment. You begin to resent others for not acknowledging or for overriding your needs and then resent yourself for not having the courage to stick up for yourself and your needs. I want you to clearly understand that you are worthy of the fulfillment of your needs; you are worthy of loving and being loved. You are worthy of being happy.

Now, I don't advocate being overassertive and overbearing in the expression of and standing up for your needs. Just as we are worthy of respect, we would do well to give others respect too. The best approach is one that empowers you to meet your needs, even while

I AM STRONG!

you help to meet the needs of others. This builds your self-worth by empowering you to feel strong and confident.

Express Your 'Self'

As a young boy and a young man, I was very keen on learning from other people. I would often mimic others as a way to gain a new talent or to impress others. I was fortunate to sometimes accompany my father as he met new people. I watched how he shook their hands, how he took a genuine interest in them, how he asked questions and participated in the conversation. In an effort to make a good first impression, I would imitate my father and was highly complimented for it. I became a sponge for interpersonal interactions and would carefully watch the people around me. I'd pick a gesture, a comment, and even body language that seemed to be both appropriate and positive, while rejecting the negative traits and gestures. This skill has helped me tremendously in all of my careers.

There is nothing wrong with mirroring and mimicking in an effort to improve yourself. However, people with low self-worth invest too much time in role-playing and pretending to be something or somebody other than who they really are. They do this by making up or exaggerating stories in order to impress those around them. When this happens these individuals find themselves behaving and acting the way others expect so they will like and accept them, while inwardly they suffer from self-indictment and self-criticism, feeling they are not good enough and, thus, need to be someone else. It is a common story about women who strike up an on-line relationship based on a profile that is mostly false, where the guy has embellished or exaggerated or simply made up things about himself to appear more appealing. I don't think there is anything wrong with trying to put your best foot forward or trying to make a good first impression; but when it goes so far as to pretend to be something you are not, you are covering up the symptom with a band-aid – trying to make up for low self-worth by puffing yourself up or putting on a mask.

It is your right, your duty, and within your power to be who you are. It is your right to express what you think, what you are feeling and how things affect you. You don't need to live up to anyone's expectations or act in such a way as to make someone proud. You have the right to say "No" when you mean no, or "I don't care," when that is what you really feel inside. Over the past several years I have come to really enjoy the reality show *The Biggest Loser*. Many of you are familiar with this television program where contestants exercise and eat healthy to lose enough weight to remain on the show for another week and the chance to win $250,000. The contestants have ranged from 200 pounds to more than 500 pounds. It took me a few seasons to really understand that it is not what you eat but what is eating you that makes the difference. The breakthrough in the show happens when the contestants finally confront the roles they have been playing and pretend to be and realize that they themselves are worth living for, that they are valuable enough to stop feeding their low self-worth with unhealthy food. I am now a big fan of the show and believe it to be one of the most inspirational shows on television.

Healthy self-worth also includes an important decision to communicate directly and state your preferences, opinions and speak in a concise and assertive voice, without being offensive or overbearing. You don't need to make excuses for your opinion or what you feel. Marta is a leader in a charity organization for mothers and their teenage daughters. In a recent meeting, Marta was leading a discussion about an upcoming activity where the young women would be making quilts and bracelets for a nursing home. As the discussion strayed from the direction it needed to go, Marta spoke up and voiced her opinion. Almost immediately she apologized for speaking up. After the meeting Marta felt ashamed and embarrassed. It wasn't that what she said was wrong or that she didn't have the right to voice her opinion. She knew all of that intellectually. Marta was mad that she apologized for it and recognized the apology for what it was: evidence of low self-esteem.

As you begin to express your 'self' respectfully to others and in a way that respects yourself, your self-worth begins to grow. You will find greater confidence in who you are. The need to exaggerate, embellish or role-play will start to diminish. Higher self-worth creates the ability to feel free to be yourself; it enables you to be who you are with all of your flaws, all of your past, all of your mistakes and anything else that you feel holds you back or makes you unappealing.

Stop Comparing

Another way to respect your needs and respect who you are is to avoid social comparisons. Making social comparisons is emotionally dangerous and can have dire effects on your well being. There will always be someone thinner, prettier, happier, smarter, who makes more money, has a better house, car or spouse. If you derive your value from external things, it is very easy to start comparing yourself to others and get caught up in a vicious cycle of being unhappy with yourself. The only real comparison is whether you are better today than yesterday.

From an early age we have been measured, graded, and pitted one against another, and most of it with good intentions. Standing in line at the supermarket, you read headlines about the prettiest people in America, how to lose weight, how to have better sex, and how to look like a movie star. At work we are subjected to relative rankings and performance scales. Our children constantly deal with scrutiny and comparisons at school: teachers grade on a curve, students discriminate who is most deserving of being in the homecoming court, and coaches pick the best athletes for MVP awards. Comparisons can come in veiled forms as well. For instance, you may feel guilty for having success when those around you are failing or have not achieved the success you have. But now that you know the difference between self-confidence and self-worth, you can see that none of those things will change who you are; they only change what you do. Sure, you may feel more confident after getting a shampoo and cut, but it does not change who you are.

Your worth is derived from a sense that you are valuable simply because you are here; simply because you live and breathe. No one is like you. Your disadvantages do not make you less of a person; your disadvantages can be your advantages! Therefore, social comparisons are an unfounded and useless activity; when you participate in social comparisons, you do your 'self' a huge disservice.

In my earlier book *The Happiness Factor: How to Be Happy No Matter What!*, I described at least three forms of comparisons that are dangerous: (1) when we compare ourselves to others; (2) when we have an unrealistic view of what success is; and (3) when we compare others to others, such as comparing your spouse, your partner, or your brother to someone else. Another example of comparing is the idea of keeping score. All of these comparisons are a form of judging the value and worth of another—a judgment that should be left to God.

Practical Tip:

When your needs are ignored, especially by yourself, you will begin to feel resentment, which will likely lead you to make some poor choices. Respect your needs by:

> Discovering your needs and writing them down.

> Learning how to communicate your needs in a way that is not interpreted as needy.

>> Educate yourself with words that express your needs better.

> Believing that you are equal to those around you, which means you are neither inferior nor superior to anyone else.

> Comparing yourself only to yourself by asking, "Am I better today than yesterday?"

> Disregarding the measuring sticks others create for you or your life.

> Learn to be truly happy for the success of others without feeling left out.

Chapter 10

O is for Own It!

Responsibility and accountability are two important aspects in growing your self-worth. The opposite of self-accountability is blame; not self-blame, but blaming others for your lack of self-worth, your low self-esteem and self-confidence. There is a reason they all start with 'self': because you own your happiness, your life experiences, your thoughts and emotions. It is time to take responsibility for where you are in life, for what you do and, most importantly, for how you value your self. All too often we allow others to determine our worth, when in reality they have nothing to do with it. Self-worth comes from the inside, not from something that someone has said or done. I entirely understand that our self-worth can be challenged when we are continually beat up, criticized, emotionally abused or denigrated. But that is all it is; it is a challenge to your self-worth, esteem and confidence, not because it is happening or has happened in the past—it is a challenge to your self-worth because you allow it to be.

Self-accountability is recognition that you own your value; no one else does. To own something means that you are going to take pride in ownership, and you will take the necessary steps to nurture, care for and maintain it. It also means that there is no one else to blame but you. Stop blaming your low self-worth on how people have treated you or what they have said. For many this is a scapegoat and a cop-out. Blaming someone else for your low self-worth means that you have nothing to do with it and, therefore, you don't have to try. To own it means for better or worse. I know that the things covered in this section will give you the tools to help improve your self-worth, but unless you have some sense of ownership, it will not matter how hard you study and use these skills; you will always come up a bit short and be subject to circumstances, situations and others to derive your value. Don't fall prey to that mentality. Step up, own it, and make it great!

There is a flip side to self-accountability. Let me use Bridget as an example. From the first client session, I recognized that Bridget had a great gift and talent. She was a very accountable person. She could be considered the poster child for accountability. But her account-ability went way beyond self-accountability to take ownership for things that didn't belong to her. This is the essence of co-depen-dence. Bridget would own her boss's problem of not having enough or the right employees. This over-accountability was demonstrated by her taking on too much work that caused her distress by disrupt-ing and contradicting her other roles, such as being a single mother and a volunteer. Bridget was out of balance, and at the core was her over-accountability. You see, accountability, like anything else, can be abused. When taken to the extreme, to be over-accountable cre-ates an impossible situation of not being able to be accountable for everything, leading to failure. That failure, if not kept in check, can damage even the strongest self-worth. Bridget derived value in ownership and accountability. The more she did, the better she felt about herself. This is a good example because Bridget was confus-ing what she did with who she was. She thought that the more she did, the more 'worthy' she was. Don't be confused; take a hard look at how you derive your value, and if your value comes from things you do, and not from inside of you, then it is time to become more self-accountable.

Here is an example of what being accountable can look like. It was only a few years ago that my wife suffered from major depression.

There were weeks where she was unable to get out of bed and face the day. It was a dark period in her life and in mine as well. With help, my wife learned to be accountable for her feelings, emotions and mental state. Rather than succumbing to lifelong depression, she learned some new skills. She learned to recognize depressing thoughts and take accountability by acknowledging, "I am having a down day," or "I am feeling low today." Soon she was able to simply say to herself, "That is a depressing thought, and I won't pay attention to it." She learned to recognize that depression was not who she was, but a controllable illness that was happening to her. By taking accountability for her feelings and emotions, she learned to have control over the illness instead of the illness controlling her.

Accepting accountability means you own it! When you own it, you are in charge of it, and that means you can change it, work with it and make it better. That is exactly what you need to do with your self-worth. Take the assessment at the end of this section to determine where you are right now; then, as the owner, take steps to improve, to truly value yourself for who you are, not what you do.

Responsibility is the companion to accountability. You may recall a quote made famous in the recent Spider Man movies, although it was actually first said by the narrator of the comic Amazing Fantasy (#15 – now worth more than $50, 000); he said, "And a lean, silent figure slowly fades into the gathering darkness, aware at last that in this world, with great power there must also come — great responsibility!" One of the greatest powers you have is the value you put on yourself – your self-worth – and thus, there is a great responsibility to care for and nurture this great power. There is power in the value you put on yourself, and how you derive that value will affect every aspect of your life for better or for worse. Self-responsibility is the concept that you alone are responsible for your happiness, and that this responsibility should not be conferred upon anyone else. There are very few of you who would deliberately give that responsibility to someone else unless you just didn't care anymore. Think about it, could you imagine someone saying to you,

"I am unable to be happy on my own; I now give you the responsibility to make me happy." It sounds absurd and even looks absurd on paper. But there are many of you that are doing just that. You let other people dictate your level of happiness. If you are treated poorly you have a choice: you can either delegate the responsibility for your happiness to that person or you can act, instead of react, and remain fully responsible for your happiness. For many of my clients there is a desire to be happy, a desire to feel fulfilled and satisfied. Yet, almost in the same breath they blame those closest to them for their lack of happiness. It is time to step up to the plate and recognize that no one is in charge of your happiness. You own it and are responsible for it.

Live Your Own Life

Who do you live for? As you think about the daily decisions and choices you make regarding where to live, what job to pursue, what's for dinner, what friends you are going to see this weekend or which side of the family you will see during the holidays, are you living the life you choose to live or are you living for someone else? Perhaps you became an accountant because your father wanted you to, when deep inside you would have preferred to become a chef. Or maybe you didn't take that trip to Europe because all of your friends thought it was irresponsible. My question is a serious one: are you living your own life or the life someone else wants you to live? Do you feel you have to live up to everyone's expectations or live a certain way to make family or friends proud of you?

As I mentioned earlier, one of my favorite reality shows on TV is *The Biggest Loser*. If you are not familiar with this inspirational show, it is a reality contest to see who of 14 to 16 contestants can lose the most weight in sixteen weeks. As I mentioned above, when it comes to weight loss and obesity, it is not what you eat but what's eating you that makes all the difference. For most of the contestants on *The Biggest Loser*, there needs to be an emotional breakthrough in order for them to really get their heads in the game. For many of the contestants, they got stuck living their life for someone else, which led to low self-worth, unhealthy eating habits, weight gain and eventual obesity. This is just one example of how living a life based on the expectations of others can create negative consequences.

The problem with living a life for someone else, on their terms and according to their expectations is that it creates serious internal conflict, resulting in resentment and anger that can destroy relationships. Remember this is not about what you do; this is about who you are. When you become someone that your father, mother, husband, boss or anyone else wants you to be, it almost always ends badly because you are not being true to yourself. I can't even begin to count the number of discussions I have had with women who, after 15 to 20 years of marriage, feel lost or feel that they have lost the life they wanted to live. None of these women would give up what they have *done*, but most of them have expressed intense feelings about waking up one day and not recognizing who they had become.

Walk into any bookstore or search on-line, and you will find thousands of books on re-inventing yourself. Why do we need to re-invent ourselves? Because we have allowed ourselves to live our life according to someone else's terms. We have allowed ourselves to become someone else. I don't think any of you need to re-invent yourself, as much as you need to re-discover who you are, what your strengths are, what your talents, gifts and contributions are, and start living your own life. The solution is to not completely disregard the expectations of others; there are times when those around us see greatness in us that we are not yet able to see. The goal is to create your own expectations, become your own best supporter, and take responsibility for who you are and who YOU want to become. Your objective is to live your own dreams and not someone else's.

Practical Tip:

Becoming accountable and responsible for your self-worth simply means that you are no longer able to blame others for your low self-worth, lack of satisfaction and happiness.

- Do not give others power over your emotions. Take charge of how you feel.

- Recognize that no person, place, or thing, can make you happy. You are responsible for your own happiness.

- Take the time to ponder and create your true life purpose so you don't live the life someone else wants.

- Own your feelings, emotions and actions by learning to forgive and let go of the past.

Chapter 11

N is for Nourish

Your self-worth is more precious than any material possession. It is worthy of nourishing and protecting. Just as a plant cannot live without sunshine, water and nutrients, your self-worth will wither away without deliberate nourishment. Unfortunately, we allow ourselves and others to step on, trample and disrespect our self-worth. It is time to take a stand and nourish the greatest gift you have been given – your self-worth.

Several years ago my wife and I bought our first house. We were so proud of this 35-year-old 1,100-square-foot home. It took us more than 10 years to save up to buy a house in Southern California. We felt it was a great personal and financial accomplishment. It felt as if we had joined the great club of home-owners across the nation. It wasn't until we started moving in that we noticed something in the hall closet. Inside the hall closet was a set of penciled-in hash marks with names and dates going back to the 1950s. I am sure you have all seen something like this, and maybe your name is next to a hash mark in your parents' home, where each year on your birthday your parents would measure how much you have grown. It was like a sentimental memento left by previous owners. We had planned on paining the interior and debated whether we should paint over the height history of the original owners of the house. In the end we decided to not paint over it but to leave it out of respect for the original owners as a symbol of growth and progress. Perhaps your height measurement is still visible in the house you grew up in.

As we examined the hash marks on the door jamb, it was easy to see that the marks only went up, not down. There was not one single year when anyone shrank in size. While you may not appreciate me stating the obvious, I want to make a significant correlation of the phenomena to your self-worth: your self-worth, the measurement of your self-worth should never shrink, it should only grow, thus requiring you to set a baseline, or in other words, to symbolically put your self-worth up against a wall and draw a mark. The question that I hope you are now asking is, "How exactly do I set a baseline? What is my starting point today?" From the time we were little, we have been trained to think of ourselves in terms of being our own worst critic. We were urged to avoid any appearance of conceit or bragging. It was made clear to us that it is better to show humility than to boast. I agree that we should demonstrate humility and refrain from boasting to others about what we do. However, remember that self-worth is about who you are, not about what you do. So the skill of setting a baseline is to be honest and objective about who you are.

To start to set a baseline, you need to ask yourself the question I ask every client: "Who are you?" Most clients respond by telling me they are a mom, a wife, an accountant or a teacher; but that is not what I want to hear, nor is it what I want them to consider. I am asking who they are to help them stop and think about who they really are. The only right answer is something positive. For example, my more religious clients eventually respond that they are "a child of God." Others finally get to the point of being able to respond similarly, "I am a wonderful and awesome human being full of gifts and talents." You see, no matter what your frame of reference, the challenge is to get down to the bare essence of who you are. Each of us can set the baseline that we are a child of a great God or that we are a marvelous creation of a great power or that we have been given a great gift to think, to act, to be. Whatever the answer, I ask my clients to reflect on their answer, to contemplate the grandeur of their being, the greatness and wonder that they are a living, vibrant, capable, intelligence full of power, light and spirit.

The next step is to ponder this and let the power of this concept grow within you. This helps you see yourself differently; no matter what has happened to you, what you have experienced, or what others may say about you, you are a wonder, a marvel, a capable and beautiful person. Set that as your baseline and, as you will learn shortly, you will need to protect it and safeguard it so that it can NEVER shrink! If you believe in God like I do, you can see the greatness in God creating you, giving you life, breath, a mind and a soul. Just as an acorn has oak DNA you have God DNA inside you. Consider the worth of that!

That alone is enough to set your baseline of self-worth. There is nothing that can diminish that; there is nothing that can take that away from you. There is no mistake, no problem, no worry or situation that can take your worth away from you. Remember, this is just a small step, you are worth so much more than I can describe here, but look into your own heart and try to see what those who love you see. Dwell on that, and let that grow within you as well. This is not boasting; this is not being conceited; this is not arrogance. This is a realization of who you are from the heart or from the inside out!

Practical Tip:

Here is something else you can try. Take a moment to fill in the blanks below with powerful adjectives that describe who you are:

I am a   (adjective 1) ,   (adjective 2) , *and*
  (adjective 3)   *woman (or man), worthy of happiness, fulfillment and satisfaction!*

Practice with different and various adjectives to create a statement that is your own and describes who you are. This now becomes your baseline, your personal statement of value and worth. Don't be too concerned if the statement is not perfect. You can certainly use different adjectives as needed. Again, this is your baseline, your stake in the ground, your immovable level of worth.

Also remember, even if you sometimes stray from this, it is still who you are, and it is who you can return to.

Silence Your Inner Critic and
Talk Tenderly to Yourself

In my book *The Happiness Factor: How to Be Happy No Matter What!*, I dedicated an entire chapter to the topic of emotional generosity. "Emotional generosity is the quality of being <u>kind</u> and <u>welcoming</u> and <u>understanding</u> of persons around you ... in all of their limitations, imperfections and flaws. Emotional generosity means that you give other human beings the benefit of the doubt, that you cut them some slack, and that you are slow to be harsh, condemning or judgmental."[6] I now want you to apply that same quality, the quality of being kind, welcoming and understanding, not just to others but to yourself as well.

Who, more than anyone else, deserves your kindness and respect? Who, more than anyone else, deserves your forgiveness? Who, more than anyone else, needs a break and the benefit of the doubt? The answer is YOU! You deserve this more than anyone else. This can be a hard thing to accept because we know more about ourselves than we know about others; we know the real truth about ourselves. So what? There is nothing you have done or could have done that makes you deserve the barrage of insults and put downs that you deliver to yourself each day. Why do affirmations work so well? Because they positively counter the negative thoughts and words we say to ourselves thousands of times a day. It is time for that to stop!

From now on it is your right, your duty, and your obligation to talk tenderly to yourself. Think of being with your best friend, consoling her after a tragedy. What would you say to her? Would you use calming and soothing words? Would you talk in hushed tones? Would you give her the benefit of the doubt? Would you tell her you have her back no matter what? Be that kind of friend to yourself. Learn to laugh at your mistakes, admit you are not perfect, and see yourself as your Creator sees you, as those who love you the most see you – you are wonderful, you are great, you are awesome. It is time to give yourself the credit you deserve.

The danger with negative self-talk is that your subconscious mind believes it and will act on that belief; those misguided actions will reinforce the belief. If you believe you are stupid, you will act stupid. If you believe you are clumsy, you will start to trip all over the place. If you believe you are unworthy of love, you will sabotage opportunities for love. What do you want your subconscious mind to believe about you? When I was growing up I had a choice of what voice I was going to listen to. I could listen to my father, who thought I was great, my step-mother, who thought I was stupid, my teachers who thought I was smart, or I could listen to myself. The loudest and most powerful voice you listen to is your own. So stop beating up on yourself. Stop scolding, criticizing, and putting yourself down. Start building yourself up.

Practical Tip:

Chose to listen to yourself only when you have something nice to say. Learn to say this: "I know that underneath all my flaws and fears, I am worthwhile and capable. From now on I will show the world more of that part of me."

Practical Tip:

Pay attention to your self-talk. If it is negative simply say, "That's not true!" The trick is to be convincing and assertive with yourself so you finally begin to realize that what you are hearing in your head is just not true!

Create a 'Criticism Filter'

Criticism is the bane of our culture—as if we have all been trained as critics, judges and jury! Whether it has to do with the clothes you wear, the kind of music you like, or the decisions you make, there is always a critic nearby to let you know how stupid it is. No matter if I am at the airport, at church, in the grocery store, walking through a mall, it seems as if I am surrounded by people who make it their business to find fault or put others down. The majority of my clients can all tell me stories of being put down, criticized and blamed, and not just at home. Bosses, supervisors, teachers, friends and co-workers took up where their immediate family left off. Critics sometimes justify their comments by calling them 'constructive' or 'instructive' criticism. There is NO such thing as constructive or instructive criticism. It took me a long time to realize this as a parent. Positive feedback will always create either positive or neutral results, where negative feedback in the form of criticism produces unpredictable results. Rarely does negative criticism have the desired effect.

For many of you I am probably being too nice about all this. I know that many of you live a nightmare of criticism day in and day out. Verbal and emotional abuse is far more prevalent than most of us realize, even among regular church-goers. It definitely can take its toll on your self-worth if you don't create a way to filter it out. In order to preserve your self-worth you need to create a criticism filter. Being the middle of seven children with a stepmother who didn't appreciate my talents and strengths, I was constantly criticized and put down. I don't believe that my childhood was that different than a lot of you experienced. My home was filled with put-downs, name calling and arguing to the point of being verbally abusive. We all took it and learned how to dish it out.

My self-awareness grew as I started to become a young man, and I found it very difficult to have any kind of positive feelings about myself. The negative voices were so loud and constant that I began to feel intense conflict. On one hand I knew that I was smart, capable and talented, but I received very little positive reinforcement. It was a mental battle to choose which voices to listen to, my own positive voice or the negative voices that surrounded me. It became so severe that I was tempted to take the easy route and give in and believe all the bad things my siblings and stepmother would say about me. At the same time, I was blessed with a vivid and lively imagination, and so I put it to work to overcome the criticism.

In my mind I created an intricate machine. The machine, more like a contraption you would see in a Dr. Seuss book, was essentially a criticism filtering machine. I won't bore you with the specific blueprint of the machine, but it worked this way: at the end of the day as I was going to bed, I would mentally invoke this machine, putting all of the negative comments I had heard throughout the day into it. Then the gears would start to move, and the machine would tear the criticisms apart, mash and grind them down. The result was that I would distill the criticism down to one or two small truths that were things I needed to improve in myself. But the majority of the residue of negative comments, now mashed and grinded by the machine, would be placed in a radioactive container and incinerated. Now, you may write this off as the fantasy of a young boy, and you are mostly right. However, the effect this had on me was so profound that I want you to experience it as well. In my naiveté I didn't realize how powerful a criticism filter is. You will find that it can be as powerful and effective for an adult as well.

Let me explain how this filtering works and why it can be so effective. Criticism is about what we *do*; it is not about who we *are*. However, most of us interpret it the other way around. Don't feel too bad about it because it's the way we have been trained, and it's likely how you are training your own children. Let me return to a previous example to help make this point. If your son or daughter were to bring home a less-than-stellar report card, what would you say? You could tell your child they are stupid and won't amount to anything; or you could express that they are smarter than that, and effort is the pathway to better grades. It is my belief that the difference between Cs and Ds, and As and Bs is not intelligence (*who you are*) but effort (*what you do*), and I'll bet you would agree with me. Thus focusing on the effort, you might give your child a pep talk about how much harder they need to work, and you might even facilitate that by taking away their cell phone and weekend privileges until their grades improve. Even if you are the most positive parent, and even if you never come close to suggesting your child isn't smart, they are going to interpret it that way. Most of us have been in similar situations and also find it difficult to separate comments about *what we do* from *who we are*. We need to resist that temptation.

Practical Tip:
When you are criticized remind yourself that it is about something you have done or something you do. It is not about who you are.

Using school grades as an example, we need to be very careful to avoid letting criticism about what we do or what we have done get interpreted to be about who we are. This is how we draw the solid line across the Self-Worth Pyramid that keeps any criticism from damaging our self-worth. You need to guard and preserve your self-worth as if were Fort Knox holding the greatest of treasures – how you feel about yourself. There is NOTHING YOU DO that should diminish your self-worth. Sure, the more you do well, the higher your self-esteem and your self-confidence will be. And that will add to your self-worth. But DO NOT LET anything you don't do well take away from how worthy you feel.

Creating your own criticism filter will become a powerful tool for you. Many of my clients have found this to be the one of the most valuable things they have learned through our sessions. The filter is helpful for another important purpose. Although we don't want to admit it, there is likely a tiny (and I do mean tiny) bit of truth in every criticism. The critic wants us to believe that it is 100% truth. However, we don't have to accept it as 100% truth. To preserve our self-worth we need to invoke a criticism filter and incinerate between 80% and 90% of it. The remaining 10% may be something you chose to work on, as you are willing and able.

Practical Tip:

In your mind, create a criticism filtering machine. You can make it as elaborate or simple as you would like. The goal is to visualize it vividly and make it functional and effective. Conjure up this machine whenever you feel criticized, and filter out 90% of all criticism.

This criticism filter that I have described can be even more useful to you when you let it operate both ways. By that I mean that not only should you filter the criticism you receive but also filter the criticism you dish out. When you start to be critical of something someone has *done,* don't interpret it to be about *who* they are. Remember that all of us make mistakes, and mistakes are seldom about who that person really is.

When does criticism become abuse? This is a question only you can answer, and it is a question that should be taken seriously. The criticism filter I have described above is not to be construed as an abuse filter. Abuse is abuse and should be treated that way. I am not advocating that you remain in an abusive relationship and rely solely upon being able to filter it out. If you think you are in an emotionally, verbally, or physically abusive relationship, I urge you to seek help. This help can come in the form of a professional trained in treatment for abuse or from a support group. Too often those who are involved in the abuse have a hard time seeing it for what it is. If the criticism filter becomes overloaded, it will not work. That will be your indicator to seek help.

Be Emotionally Generous with Your 'Self'

I spoke earlier about emotional generosity as it relates to talking tenderly to yourself. Now I want you to apply that same principle to give your 'self' a break; to cut your 'self' some slack; and to be kind, welcoming and understanding to yourself without being self-judging or self-indicting. Because self-worth is about who you are and not what you do, it is time to put what you do into perspective. By making separating who you are from what you do, you are able to look at yourself and acknowledge your strengths, weaknesses, mistakes and errors in judgment objectively, while at the same time accepting yourself as worthy and worthwhile. It is dangerous to derive value from what you do because you can't be perfect, nor can you be the very best at everything you try. If your self-value is dependent on how well you do something, you will always be faced with disappointment. To increase your self-worth, you must create a healthy perspective about your mistakes, blunders, obstacles, setbacks and apparent failures. One way to do this is to be emotionally generous with yourself. Don't interpret temporary and specific setbacks as permanent and general. It is always better to consider experience from the perspective of what you have learned, rather than what has happened to you.

Preserve, Protect and Affirm your Great Worth

Each one of us has that one special thing that we cherish above all else. It could be a diamond necklace, your wedding ring, a car, or a plaque in recognition of some achievement, regardless of what it is, think of how much time you spend preserving and protecting it. You should have even more care and concern over preserving and protecting your self-worth. Earlier, I had you draw a hard line across the Self-Worth Pyramid, a barrier that will not let any criticism in to damage or diminish your self-worth. That is just one way of preserving and protecting your self-worth. Your baseline self-worth should never diminish, but should only increase and become stronger and healthier. The healthier it is, the better you can handle life's drama, stress, trials and other negatives.

As a father of young children, I did my best to protect them as they grew up. As they began to walk, I was there to make sure that they didn't hurt themselves when they fell. As they grew older, my protection was not so much physical as it was mental, moral and emotional. That is the same protection you need to create for your self-worth. Treat it as if it is precious and special. The age-old schoolyard mantra is as true today as it once was, "Sticks and stones may break my bones, but words can never hurt me." You must remember that it is your choice to not let any symbolic 'name calling' diminish your self-worth. You do this by taking the higher road, choosing to act and not react, and by applying the principles covered in this book.

Affirming your self-worth is another way to nurture the health of your self-worth. You affirm your self-worth by acting in accordance with your beliefs. If you believe you are a strong, capable and beautiful woman, then act like it. If you act like you are a strong, capable and beautiful woman, then believe it. Affirm your self-worth by walking the talk.

Practical Tip:

In order for something to be healthy and grow, it needs to be nourished.

- ❯ You are the only one who can reject you – SO DON'T DO IT!
- ❯ Create and use a criticism filter.
  - ❯ Practice the words, "That was mean and hurtful, and I choose to ignore what you just said." You may also want to add, "I have too much self-respect to accept your lack of respect."
- ❯ Talk more tenderly to yourself using words you would use when you speak to someone you have the utmost respect for.
- ❯ Protect your self-worth by not letting feedback about *what you do* be interpreted to be about *who you are.*

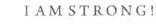

Chapter 12

G is for Genuine

To be genuine is to be authentic or real. Authenticity is a self-worth builder; conversely, being inauthentic (false or imitation) tears your self-worth down. A few years ago my family relocated from Boise, Idaho to Mesa, Arizona. The climate was not the only difference we had to deal with. After being in Arizona for about a year, I noticed some 'tracks' on the wall in the garage that looked like mud. I didn't pay too much attention to it until I saw the same tracks in my neighbor's garage. I mentioned that I had the same funny tracks. My neighbor was quite serious when he told me that those tracks mean you have termites! I had termites in my garage! Termites are a silent destroyer, and unless you take care of them quickly, they can cause significant damage and compromise the structural integrity of your home. The same is true when you are not genuine. Being disingenuous is a silent destroyer of your self-worth.

You are genuine when your actions, words, and thoughts are aligned. But when you are living your life in such a way so as to please someone else or to make someone proud of you, there is a chance you are not living as authentically as you should. When we adjust our actions simply to please someone or be liked, to make us look good, or win approval, we soon begin to resent that person and ourselves because we are diminishing our self-worth in the process of being disingenuous. A classic example of this is the young man who goes to college to be a doctor because that is what is father does or expects, while in his heart he wants to be a musician. It may happen soon, or it may take several years, but inevitably, this young man will realize that he is not being genuine; he must change his motivation or his career, or pursue both, in order to remain genuine.

Being truly genuine is difficult because small inauthentic choices are easy to justify. Although a man may never cheat on his wife, he may convince himself that it is ok to steal from his employer or cheat on his taxes. A woman who would never lie to a friend may find it easy to lie to her employer, calling in sick when, indeed, she is quite well. These seemingly small inauthentic behaviors are like a cancer that will infect your self-worth and impact the power that high self-worth can have in your life. A strong indicator of being disingenuous is fear of being 'found out.' The only people who live in fear of being found out are those who are living a lie, no matter how large or how small.

Being afraid that someone will learn the truth about you is a very aggressive cancer affecting your self-worth. Here is an example: Sheryl came to me for motivation and success coaching. She had an intense feeling that she was treading water and that she just couldn't get ahead at work and in life. She kept trying and trying. She said, "I just can't seem to get it right. It is as if I reach a certain point, and then I sabotage myself. I can't seem to keep a boyfriend, and I can't seem to get ahead at work. It is like some invisible wall is always there blocking my progress." It wasn't until our fifth session that I discovered that Sheryl had a few secrets. Sheryl's lies and secrets created a terrible fear of being 'found out.'

The secrets that Sheryl kept had infected her self-worth and created a lack of self-confidence at work, especially when she would apply for a promotion or a new job. Sheryl had lied on her resume. Her exact words were, "I exaggerated a few of my accomplishments." The truth is that Sheryl was just three credits away from graduating with her Bachelor's degree, but on her resume she stated she had already graduated. To some, this may seem like a tiny white lie that is understandable or easy to justify. But your self-worth is quite sensitive, and a lie like that is like sleeping on an air mattress that has a slow leak – it's not too noticeable when you first lie down, but over time it becomes quite uncomfortable.

The other secret was that Sheryl got pregnant as a teenager and gave her child up for adoption. In her heart she knew she did the right thing. But Sheryl lived in fear that someone, particularly the men she dated, would find out and judge her poorly. This fear of being 'found out' created a barrier to intimacy. Each time a relationship would progress to a point of deepening emotional closeness, she would back away, feeling unable to share her past.

Sheryl needed to repair these inauthenticities in her life. It was easier than she had imagined. The lie on her resume was easily corrected by enrolling in the class she needed to graduate and adjusting her resume to reflect the truth until she completed the course. As for her past, that was solved as she applied the skills found in Part 4 of this book about overcoming your past.

Your self-worth has great power: power to enable you to overcome trauma, change, relationship issues and other problems. Don't reduce that power by living a disingenuous life. It may mean that you need to take action to return to authenticity and to re-build your self-worth. That will in turn grow your self-esteem and increase your self-confidence.

Don't Deflect Compliments

Be genuine when you are given a compliment. How well you handle compliments is another indicator of high or low self-worth. When you receive a compliment, are you able to accept the compliment or do you feel compelled to deflect the compliment in some way? For instance, say you wore a nice but older dress to a party. If someone were to mention how nice your dress is, do you simply say thank you or do you deflect by saying, "Oh, this old thing?" Deflecting minimizes the compliment and could offend the giver. It is an indicator of how you feel about yourself, not a reflection of how you feel about the dress.

Your ability to graciously accept a compliment is directly related to how you feel about yourself. So often I witness people minimizing or dismissing a sincere compliment when it is given. Are we afraid of success? Do we think that we don't deserve recognition? Many of us are afraid of appearing arrogant and dismiss compliments, as if to appear humble. However, dismissing a compliment diminishes the intent of the person giving the compliment. Because of my speaking and consulting engagements, I am often told how well I do. At first I would dismiss the compliment with some quip or comment that spoiled the intent of the person. I have since learned that the most appropriate response to any compliment or expression of appreciation is to simply say, "Thank you," or "Thank you, I appreciate you saying that."

Another indicator of the health of your self-worth is your ability to give sincere compliments. A person with higher self-worth is able to give honest and sincere compliments without feeling as if they are diminishing their own value. It is always curious to me how much we, as a culture, withhold compliments because of fear: fear of being brash, fear of having our intentions misinterpreted, or the fear of feeling less than the person we are complimenting. For instance, if a man were to approach a woman and express how attractive she is, his compliment may come across as a come-on instead of a sincere compliment. However, we shouldn't let that stop us from expressing appreciation and giving compliments or giving credit where and when credit is due. Certainly we should never feel as if a compliment takes away from who we are or how we feel about ourselves. I realize that this may be hard for you if you suffer from low self-worth, but I challenge you to try to be more complimentary. It will not only make someone's day, it will make you feel better as well.

Practical Tip:

Your self-worth will grow by leaps and bounds as you live authentically. This genuineness will impact your life in numerous ways and affect those around you for good. Here are some tips on how to be genuine with yourself:

 ❱ Be honest in all of your dealings and relationships. It is better to be silent than to lie.

 ❱ Learn to be diplomatic in your communications.

 ❱ Reply with a sincere "thank you" to any compliment, big or small.

 ❱ Express appreciation through giving genuine compliments to others.

 ❱ Don't lie to yourself through self-criticism, and don't exaggerate your weaknesses.

 ❱ Give yourself a break when you do something wrong or misbehave. Admit the wrong, resolve to do better and move on.

 ❱ Be emotionally generous with yourself and others.

I AM STRONG!

Chapter 13

Putting the
I AM STRONG Formula
into Action

So far we have covered a lot of ground in setting the foundation for understanding self-worth and how self-worth is the basis of self-esteem and self-confidence. By putting the principles in this section into action, your self-worth will definitely grow. I have had clients who, within a few short weeks, barely remember the weak and fearful person they had become. If you already have a functioning self-worth, the change you feel may not be as dramatic as for those who were struggling intensely. But trust in and practice the I AM STRONG formula, and you will experience the power it will give you to face life with greater optimism, feel better about yourself and your circumstances, interact with others with greater confidence, and experience the peace that comes from knowing you are worthy of greatness because you simply *are*.

Here is a review with a few suggestions to put I AM STRONG to work for you:

Identify: Take a good look at where your self-worth is now and where you derive your value. Pay attention to indicators of the health of or choices that may be affecting your self-worth. Observe yourself without self-indictment.

Acknowledge and Accept: You are who you are. It does you no good to continue wishing you were someone else. Acknowledge your weaknesses without letting them define you. This will help you move beyond denial and on to action. It is perfectly fine to want to improve, but accept that you are great, you are worthy, and grow from there.

Minimize your Weaknesses and Maximize your Strengths: We all have weaknesses. Don't let yourself be defined by them. Learn to see your weaknesses for what they are, an opportunity for growth and learning. Put your focus on your strengths.

Practice Self-Recognition: It is ok to pat yourself on the back and celebrate your accomplishments and successes. You can be pleased with yourself and still be humble and modest. Learn to recognize whether or not you are dependent on praise, recognition or validation from others. Break dependency by validating yourself. It is time to recognize that you are smart, capable, beautiful and wonderful even if no one tells you so. Don't compare yourself to anyone but yourself.

Be True to You: Have faith in your ability to keep your promises. Break free from indecision, and move forward doing the best you can. There are very few decisions you make that are life-threatening, so make decisions with confidence, and know you are capable of making it right.

Respect Your Needs: If your own emotional needs are suppressed, they will eventually break free of their prison and cause you to overreact and misbehave. We all have needs. It is now time for you to respect and communicate those needs without blaming others for not recognizing them or fulfilling them. Don't assume that others know your needs unless you have communicated them. You may need to research and learn words and phrases that effectively express feelings.

Own It! Take responsibility for your own emotional destiny and for the path you are on. Stop the blame game, and realize that no one but you is responsible for your self-worth and happiness. This should be liberating, as you realize that you are in control! You can change how you feel about yourself.

Nourish your Self-Esteem: Don't participate in activities or thoughts that are destructive to your self-worth. Your self-worth will grow as you talk tenderly to yourself, filter out unwanted and destructive criticism, give yourself a break and the benefit of the doubt.

Be Genuine: Be real, be genuine, be honest, and be your best. Articulate your core beliefs and moral values, and stand up for them. Be sincere in your relationships. Stray from doing things only because you are obligated to do so. Live with authenticity.

When it comes to your self-worth, the bottom line is this: you should give yourself more credit because you are more than worth it! YOU ARE STRONG!

Your Self-Worth Inventory and Assessment

For each question below,
answer on a scale from 1 – disagree to 10 – agree.

1	I like the way I look.
	Disagree 1 2 3 4 5 6 7 8 9 10 Agree

2	When I think about my accomplishments, I have a sense of pride.
	Disagree 1 2 3 4 5 6 7 8 9 10 Agree

3	Other people like being around me.
	Disagree 1 2 3 4 5 6 7 8 9 10 Agree

4	When I make a mistake, I am quick to forgive myself.
	Disagree 1 2 3 4 5 6 7 8 9 10 Agree

5	I am satisfied with my chosen profession.
	Disagree 1 2 3 4 5 6 7 8 9 10 Agree

6	When I can't solve a problem, I am confident that I will learn from the experience and do better next time.
	Disagree 1 2 3 4 5 6 7 8 9 10 Agree

7	When I can't solve a problem, I am comfortable asking for help.
	Disagree 1 2 3 4 5 6 7 8 9 10 Agree

8	I often try new things.
	Disagree 1 2 3 4 5 6 7 8 9 10 Agree

9	I like and feel comfortable meeting new people.
	Disagree 1 2 3 4 5 6 7 8 9 10 Agree

10	I love myself.
	Disagree 1 2 3 4 5 6 7 8 9 10 Agree

11	I am able to listen to and accept criticism from others without it ruining my day.
	Disagree 1 2 3 4 5 6 7 8 9 10 Agree

12	I am able to make a mistake without feeling like a failure.										
	Disagree	1	2	3	4	5	6	7	8	9	10 Agree
13	I avoid comparing myself to others.										
	Disagree	1	2	3	4	5	6	7	8	9	10 Agree
14	My opinion counts, even if it is not expressed.										
	Disagree	1	2	3	4	5	6	7	8	9	10 Agree
15	I accept responsibility for my actions, as well as my reactions to what others say about me.										
	Disagree	1	2	3	4	5	6	7	8	9	10 Agree
16	I do not put myself down or practice self-criticism.										
	Disagree	1	2	3	4	5	6	7	8	9	10 Agree
17	I am able to be around people who may criticize me without feeling uncomfortable.										
	Disagree	1	2	3	4	5	6	7	8	9	10 Agree
18	I can handle whatever is put in front of me.										
	Disagree	1	2	3	4	5	6	7	8	9	10 Agree
19	My actions make a difference in this world.										
	Disagree	1	2	3	4	5	6	7	8	9	10 Agree
20	I comfortably accept and give recognition and compliments.										
	Disagree	1	2	3	4	5	6	7	8	9	10 Agree

Add the score from each of the 20 questions: _____

A score of 100 or more means you likely have a healthy view of yourself and a good foundation of self-worth. Applying the I AM STRONG formula may improve your well-being even more.

A score of 99 or below indicates that that you would benefit from purposely investing in your self-worth. Be reassured that there is great hope for your improved happiness and self-worth by practicing the principles in the I AM STRONG formula!

I AM STRONG!

Part 3:

The Miracles of
Authentic Forgiving

I AM STRONG!

My niece, Madasin, loves reptiles. Not just any reptiles, she loves lizards and even keeps a bearded dragon lizard as a pet. This lizard goes almost everywhere that Madasin goes. Reptiles, snakes, lizards and the like are not my favorite animals. I certainly would not keep one as a pet. It is a marvel to me that Madasin seems right at home with reptiles of all kinds. Those of you who have spent any time around lizards will know something quite interesting about them: they shed their skin. Younger lizards grow much faster and shed their skin more often than older lizards. The shedding can range from every 4 to 6 weeks, to twice a year.

Lizards shed their skin in order to grow. If a lizard is unable to shed due to issues with diet, housing, humidity, temperature and other variables, he is likely to die. Additionally, if the shed is incomplete, particularly around the toes, legs and spines, it can result in auto-amputation. Lizards must shed to grow. Like lizards, we too need to shed in order to grow. We need to shed our bad habits and emotional burdens. Shedding your bad habits and emotional burdens will bolster your self-worth and improve your self-esteem and self-confidence. Authentic forgiving is a process of shedding negative emotional baggage that we wear like an old heavy skin. Like the lizards, unless we shed, there are negative consequences that may not be as gruesome as auto-amputation, but can be just as potentially devastating.

After a recent seminar, Kimberly lingered so she could tell me her story. A few months prior, she read my book *The Happiness Factor: How to Be Happy No Matter What!* She took the chapter on forgiveness seriously enough to do something about it. She explained that for eight years she had not talked to Suzanne, a friend since pre-school. So much time had passed that Kimberly couldn't even remember what caused the ill feelings, but she still carried an emotional burden that was heightened each time she thought of Suzanne. After reading the chapter on forgiveness, Kimberly decided to reach out to Suzanne and make amends. Although it was hard, she did it and was happy to tell me that their friendship has been renewed and is growing. Eight years? Can you imagine hanging on to ill feelings for eight years? I was both touched by the progress and saddened that Kimberly had not found the miracles of forgiving much sooner.

Kimberly is not alone; I would imagine that many of you harbor ill feelings toward someone who has hurt you, abused you, rejected you, or shamed and embarrassed you. Perhaps there is a family member with whom you have not spoken in years because of a past offense. There can be a lot of pain associated with this topic, and in no way do I want to minimize the pain you have felt or are feeling at this moment. However, you don't have to feel that way any longer. There is a saying, that "withholding forgiveness is like drinking a deadly poison, hoping to harm another." Another saying is, "Withholding forgiveness is like picking up a hot coal with the intention of throwing it at the person who has hurt or offended you." These quotes are quite accurate, in that withholding forgiveness harms you more than it hurts the offender. If you still feel anger, pain and sorrow when you think of the person or people who betrayed, offended, embarrassed or hurt you, this is the effect of holding on to that coal or drinking that poison. You can heal and free yourself of those painful feelings.

This section focuses on you and the knowledge and skills you need to authentically forgive so you can shed the emotional burdens you carry. It is not my intention to spend a lot of time discussing forgiveness from a theoretical or religious point of view. In this part of the book, the focus will be on *forgiving* as something in which you will actively engage, rather than waiting for someone to say they are sorry or waiting to be forgiven. You cannot control another person, and no matter how much you may want to, you cannot inflict as much pain on your offender as you feel. It is time to shed that old painful skin and enjoy the new skin of peace, emotional freedom and power.

Forgiving is not just reserved for big issues, big problems, or just when you are hurt the most. Neither is forgiving a once-in-a-while activity. As we discuss forgiving, keep in mind that it applies to the little things in life as much as it applies to the big things. Certainly, the effort you would put into forgiving your spouse for infidelity will be more intense than forgiving your spouse for leaving socks on the floor. Both are worthy of your willingness to forgive. Learning how to rid yourself of the pain and negative emotions will free you to receive greater happiness and love. Perhaps there are things you consider so bad that you could never forgive. If so, I would ask you to reconsider. I assert that there is nothing so great, so onerous or so bad that you can never forgive or heal. It may take a more sincere effort, but as you will soon learn, forgiving is more about you and your emotional well-being than it is about your offender.

I AM STRONG!

Chapter 14

Better or Bitter?

Previously, I covered the topic of self-awareness as an important step in developing a healthy self-worth. Self-awareness is also important as you reflect on how you typically respond when you are offended, misunderstood, unfairly treated, sinned against, falsely accused, disrespected, passed over, rejected or hurt by those who are supposed to love you. Is your typical response to become bitter, vengeful, angry or withdrawn? Do you seethe and plot ways to get back at that person, or do you treat them as if they are dead to you? Or is your typical response that of love, reaching out in compassion and trying to resolve the problem in order to rid yourself of the burden? Becoming aware of how you respond when hurt or offended can give you needed insight into the importance of this topic for you. The nature of your response to the situations named above determines the nature and quality of your life.

I'm sure you have heard that "time heals all wounds." I disagree with that statement; while time can lessen the intensity of a wound, it certainly does not always heal it. And in the meantime, you feel miserable while you're waiting. Why not learn how to accelerate the time between the offense and authentic forgiving? Instead of feeling hurt and pain for weeks, months, years, and even a lifetime, you can learn how to respond in a way that removes the pain and restores positive emotions, even love, as expressed in The Prayer of Saint Francis of Assisi:

Lord, make me an instrument of thy peace.
Where there is hatred, let me sow love;
Where there is injury, pardon;
Where there is doubt, faith;
Where there is despair, hope;
Where there is darkness, light;
Where there is sadness, joy.

This prayer represents the goal of authentic forgiving – to restore peace where there is hurt, and pardon where there is injury. The choice is yours. You can feel misery or you can authentically forgive the person who has offended you, including yourself, and do it in a way that maintains your dignity and bolsters your self-worth, self-esteem and self-confidence.

Who Deserves Your Forgiveness the Most?

Think about all the people who have offended, hurt, betrayed or disrespected you—a schoolyard friend, a teacher, a parent, neighbor, boss or coworker, a stranger or a family member. Regardless of who these people are, which one of them deserves your forgiveness the most? I admit that this is a bit of a trick question because the answer is none of them and all of them. But an even more correct answer is you! You deserve your forgiveness more than anyone else. I realize that this may be a hard concept for some of you, but it is the truth. This actually becomes a simple concept after you have mastered the principles presented in Part 1 of this book. As you increase your self-worth, you quickly realize that you are worthy of being forgiven by yourself first and then by anyone whom you have offended or hurt. As we continue to discuss the miracles of forgiving, let me be crystal clear, all of these principles apply first to you and then to others. As I mentioned earlier, you cannot give away what you do not have. If you cannot forgive yourself, then the forgiveness you give to others is minimized and somewhat inauthentic. No matter what you have done, no matter whom you have offended, no matter how serious the offense may seem, you can and should forgive yourself. First and fore-most, you deserve your forgiveness the most.

I was surprised when Daniel confided in me that he had served time in prison for causing an accident while driving drunk. He killed a young man who was about to graduate from high school and severely injured the man's younger sister. Daniel told me, "My sincere effort to be forgiven by the family of the young man is nothing compared to the effort to forgive myself. I am finally at a point where I can truly forgive myself. It doesn't change anything that I did, but it helps me live in peace despite what I have done." It has been a long hard road for Daniel to learn to forgive himself, but he is making great progress. And so can you! If he can do it, you can too!

Forgiving brings untold miracles into your life. Forgive is a verb; it connotes action and requires that you 'do' something. At Amazon. com alone, there are more than 3000 books on the subject of forgiv-ing and forgiveness, ranging from the secular to the religious. There is also a growing body of research on forgiving and its effects. Some psychologists even use forgiveness therapy to overcome emotional issues, such as depression. There are also studies in which forgive-ness therapy with heart surgery patients demonstrates a higher rate of healing among those who actively forgive.[7] Forgiving is found in most of the world religions as a way of pleasing God or simply doing the right thing.

There is a strong Christian belief that we must forgive others in order to be forgiven by God. As a rule Christians and non-Christians alike believe that forgiveness is worthwhile and necessary. However, in one university study, it was found that out of more than 200 Christian and non-Christian college students, a majority of the non-Christians stated that an apology is necessary as a condition of forgiveness. Only a small percentage of the Christian students (15.6%) felt the same way.[8] If you are waiting for an apology before you forgive, you might be waiting a long time. Authentic forgiving is not based on apologies. Don't wait; don't be in pain any longer. If for no other reason than to rid yourself of pain, forgive *now*, no matter who it is. If you were to go to the doctor for minor surgery and the doctor made a mistake that ended up causing you to experience terrible pain, would you stop taking pain killers until the doctor apologized? I doubt it. Waiting for someone to apologize before forgiving them is doing the same thing.

To this point, Dr. Sidney Simon, a recognized authority on forgiving, gives an excellent definition of forgiving: *"Forgiveness is freeing up and putting to better use the energy once consumed by holding grudges, harboring resentments, and nursing unhealed wounds. It is rediscovering the strengths we always had and relocating our limitless capacity to understand and accept other people and ourselves."* Freeing ourselves from the emotional pain should be reason enough to forgive.

The Impact of Withholding Forgiveness

Withholding forgiveness creates heavy emotional baggage we carry around with us that includes the following:

> Anger

> Fear

> Ultra-sensitivity, resulting in being easily offended

> Physical and emotional illness

> Spiritual stagnation

> Loneliness

> Victimization

> Being overly judgmental of others

> Fear of being hurt, rejected, or disrespected

> Resentment

> Bitterness

> Lower self-worth, self-esteem and self-confidence

Are you experiencing any of these consequences right now? In all my years as a life coach, whether my clients are couples needing help in their relationship, a client needing help to find meaning and purpose in her life, or a client wanting motivation and success coaching, it has been my experience that withholding forgiveness is almost always a barrier to happiness, success and fulfillment. The consequences of withholding forgiveness can have specific physiological effects, such as increased blood pressure and hormonal changes. It has also been linked to cardiovascular disease, immune system suppression, and possibly impaired neurological function and memory. Think of the kind of life you want to live, a life of peace, emotional confidence, and freedom from hurt, pain and sorrow—you will have a much better chance of living that kind of life through honest and sincere effort to forgive. One study examined 20 individuals in happy relationships, compared with 20 in troubled relationships. The latter had higher baseline levels of cortisol, a hormone associated with impaired immune system function—which shot up even farther when they were asked to think about their relationships. "It happens down the line, but every time you feel unforgiving, you are more likely to develop a health problem," says Everett Worthington, executive director of A Campaign for Forgiveness Research, a non-profit organization that supports research into forgiving.[9]

Withholding forgiveness is a choice you make; you have it within you to make a better choice. I am always surprised when I receive clients who are passionate about changing their lives and willing to do what it takes to remove the obstacles to that happiness…that is, until it comes to forgiving those who have offended them. If you want to experience peace, happiness, joy and feel better about yourself, then stop withholding forgiveness. Let the barriers to your joy and happiness come tumbling down.

I AM STRONG!

Chapter 15

What is Forgiving?

Before we get too much further into this section on the miracles of forgiving, let's come to understanding about what forgiving is and what it is not. This becomes an important exercise because the common misconceptions about forgiving can present barriers to healing and happiness.

Forgiving is not:

❯ **A face-to-face confrontation.** Forgiving does not require you to meet face-to-face and confront your offender. There may be other reasons for doing this, and many of them are quite positive; but don't think you have to confront the person to forgive them. Depending on the situation, a face-to-face meeting could make things worse.

❯ **Just a feeling.** Yes, forgiving does include feelings and emotions, but it is more than that. It is important to feel forgiving, but it also requires you to do something. That something may be emotional action or it may include a verbalization of your forgiveness to God or your higher power. It is more than just a feeling.

❯ **Letting someone off the hook.** This is a tremendously important point! When you forgive someone, it does not mean they are no longer accountable for their actions, and it certainly does not let them off the hook. Not that long ago I had a client who was abused by her father for many years. She can forgive him and should forgive him for all of the benefits that I will discuss later, but it is not an act of condoning or absolving his actions. You can forgive to release your emotional pain, but that does not release the other person from consequences, retribution or the need to make restitution.

> **Immediately trusting the other person.** Forgiving the person who has offended or sinned against you does not mean you have to be their best friend. In fact, in situations where trust has been lost, you can't and shouldn't immediately put full trust in this person. Trust is conditional; when trust is lost, it must be earned again through demonstrated trustworthy behavior sustained over time. Trust and forgiving are mutually exclusive. Forgiving is about you, about how you feel, about doing what is necessary for you to feel at peace. You don't have to let this person back into your life. Only do that when it is the right thing to do for the right reasons, not just because you have forgiven them.

> **Expecting an apology.** Forgiving is the right thing to do period! It does not matter whether that person has apologized or not. Sincere apologies are wonderful, but infrequent. Don't wait. Forgive now. Because forgiving does not require a face-to-face, voice-to-voice, or even email correspondence, you can forgive now. If an apology comes, you will welcome it and cherish it. But don't wait for it, and don't condition your forgiveness on an apology.

> **Waiting for someone to get what they deserve.** Even at an early age we have a sense that there is a place for justice. We all want to see justice being served by offenders being punished. Whether in the home, school, or community and world as reported in the media, we love it and feel safer when good

prevails over evil. However, in real life, offenders don't often get what they deserve immediately. Take this out of the forgiveness equation. You can seek justice with a forgiving heart.

》 **Waiting for time to heal our wounds.** Time is not a healer. Time is just time, and yes, the intensity of your pain may subside as you realize that you are still a great person, even if you have been offended or hurt. Time can also be a great deceiver, making you think that everything is ok, when indeed it is not. Don't get stuck in this rationalization. The sooner you forgive, the sooner you can start to break down barriers and obstacles to true happiness and joy.

Forgiving is:

》 **The greatest gift you can give yourself.** No matter who has wronged you, even if it is you yourself, forgiving is one of the greatest gifts you can give. I want you to consider that forgiving is not about the other person. It is about you. It is about creating positive emotions and reducing negative emotions, both of which lead to peace and happiness. The minute you think this is about the offender, you have given that person the power to steal peace and happiness from you. Don't delegate that power to anyone.

》 **A personal choice.** It is a choice to forgive and to begin the healing process. Whether it is something small or something big, you cannot fully heal until you forgive. Forgiving is still a choice, even if you may feel compelled to forgive because of your religious or spiritual beliefs.

》 **Prioritizing healing over being right.** You may be justified in all of your thinking about fairness and accountability, but forgiving is not about fairness or waiting until someone has paid their debt or suffered a penance. Forgiving is prioritizing your emotional health over being right. The choice is simple: be miserable and be right, or forgive and be happy.

> **A journey of growth, giving, and understanding.** Forgiving, as I will explain later, is a process that can be considered a personal journey of self-development. For those of us who are Christian, forgiving is a God-like thing to do and brings us closer to God as we become like him. It takes courage to forgive. Be courageous.

> **An act of charity.** In my last book, *The Happiness Factor: How to Be Happy No Matter What!*, I dedicated an entire chapter to the topic of emotional generosity. Emotional generosity is one act of giving of who you are (kindness, understanding, love, etc...), not just of what you have. Forgiving is ultimately an act of personal charity.

> **Merciful.** Forgiving, especially when the other person is unrepentant, unremorseful, and has not apologized, is an act of mercy, almost to the point of disregarding justice. You don't need to wait until the offender has paid his price; you can forgive now. Forgiving requires you to see them in their innocence instead of their guilt and to answer injustice with mercy.

> **A decision to remove yourself from being judge, jury and punisher.** To a certain degree, by not forgiving you are electing yourself as judge, jury and punisher. Some people even take it so far as to appoint themselves as the offender's probation officer, keeping track of and adding every offense to their already offensive rap sheet. Forgiving is releasing yourself from those positions and having faith that, either in the short run or the long run, the offender will have to pay a price. The longer you fret over whether the offender is being punished, the longer you will be in pain. You can still pursue legal or civil action aggressively, even if you have forgiven. Forgiving does not let the offender off the hook. It is a means of helping you let go and let God, the ultimate and perfect judge, heal you. Forgiving is surrendering it to Him.

I AM STRONG!

If Withholding Forgiveness is so Bad, Why is Forgiving so Hard to Do?

Let's face it, forgiving is not easy. When it comes to forgiving ourselves, we may find it extremely hard because we know the whole story; we know our intent, our motivations, and the outcome. We may try, but we can't hide from ourselves. Masking the event, blocking it out, or pretending it didn't happen only creates intense internal conflict. Lack of resolution often results in further misbehavior. Perhaps we are so guilt-ridden and have felt guilty for so long that it has become our normal. You may also mistakenly believe that what you have done requires you to suffer as part of your penance; you may think that until you reach some magical milestone of suffering, you can't and won't forgive yourself. Not forgiving yourself is akin to self-abuse.

Forgiving others is equally difficult. We may withhold forgiveness until our offender apologizes adequately; and while we wait, we suffer. It may also be hard to forgive because the offensive or abusive behavior is still ongoing. Admittedly, it is hard to forgive someone for offenses that persist; it is one thing to forgive what's in the past, and it's another to forgive what is still happening in the present. We may also feel as if we have no need to forgive because we have already dealt with the hurtful behavior or event in some way. This happened to me. When I was eight years old my mother abandoned me. She sent my brother, sister and I to the store; when we came back she was gone. I didn't see her again for many years and had only seen her six times by the time I turned 48. So much time had passed that I considered the event over; I thought I had already dealt with it and didn't need to formally forgive her. I was wrong! The effects of not formally forgiving her had become my normal, and it wasn't until I made a sincere effort to forgive her that I felt unburdened, as if darkness had left me. You can think of a lot of reasons why you shouldn't forgive someone, and some of the reasons will be justified. But there is not one reason that is worth you continuing to carry the pain.

Several years ago my family vacationed near Payette Lake in McCall, Idaho. It is a pristine mountain lake with hiking, camping and water sports. During this vacation I was relaxing on the beach, when I saw a father carrying his 10-year-old daughter. Shortly after he set her down in the sand and went off to fetch something, I smelled something terrible and putrid. I looked at the young girl and noticed a terrible burn on her leg. The burn was about six inches long by four inches wide of raw flesh in the middle, blackened on the edges. I winced, thinking of the pain she must be in; yet, she showed no signs of pain. I asked her, "Can I help you? That burn looks nasty, are you taking something for the pain?" She responded that she could feel no pain, that she was paralyzed from the waist down. She explained that she was riding a jet ski with her father and her leg had fallen on to the exhaust. "Because I can't feel anything in my legs, I didn't know I was being burned until we could smell it," she said. Fortunately, she quickly got the medical attention she needed to prevent an infection. The ability to feel pain may not seem a good thing, but it serves an important purpose, as you can see. Like physical pain, emotional pain is an indicator that something is wrong and we need to take action. All too often we hear of people who numb their emotional pain with drugs, alcohol or other destructive behaviors. You don't need to do that! When you feel emotional pain, take action! When you feel offended, guilty, remorseful, bitter, angry or any other emotional pain, let there be a glaring alarm that goes off in your head saying – ACT NOW!

Chapter 16

Forgiving Pays Huge Dividends

I don't think that any of you would argue that flossing your teeth is a good thing to do. The benefits of flossing your teeth far outweigh the drawbacks. Flossing your teeth at least once a day can help reduce bad breath and plaque buildup, prevent cavities, decrease your chances of getting gum disease, and reduce your trips to the dentist. Even with all of those benefits, only about 33% of the U.S. population flosses on a regular basis. Why? Mostly because we simply have not made it a habit! Also, most people believe that the worst consequences of not flossing are so far into the future that there is no immediate need for it. So living with bad breath becomes normal; it feels more comfortable than beginning a new habit of regular flossing. Similarly, living with emotional pain feels so normal for some of you that peace and happiness might feel uncomfortable. I am not saying that you don't appreciate feeling peace and happiness, but once you do feel it, you immediately start to think about what will go wrong, and that throws you right back into that emotional pain that feels comfortable because you've become used to living with it. However, if you strongly consider one or more of the benefits of forgiving, perhaps it will strike you as something you want to strive for. Perhaps a desire will stir within you to take forgiving seriously enough to make it something you do every single day. Forgiving as a daily practice offers you the following benefits:

> **Spiritual integrity**: Forgiving ourselves allows us to see the good in ourselves, which enables us to see the good in others.

When we forgive ourselves, we WANT to forgive others. In this way, we walk the talk. Spiritual integrity enables you to have more confidence in your relationship with God. You are able to trust yourself more, which leads you to trust God more.

》 **Deeper, stronger love for all people**: Withholding forgiveness is one of the great barriers to getting along with your spouse or others, especially when it comes to the little things. Forgiving removes the barriers to feeling and giving deep and true love in all of your relationships. I have seen this increase of love with many of the couples I have coached. When each person is finally truly willing and able to forgive the other person, the magic of true love starts to blossom again.

》 **Higher self-worth, self-esteem and self-confidence**: A huge benefit of forgiving yourself and others is the boost it gives to your self-worth, which leads to a higher self-esteem and greater self-confidence. When you forgive yourself, you are demonstrating that you are worthy of forgiveness, happiness and peace. That peace with yourself will lead you to want to protect and preserve your self-worth by forgiving others.

》 **Greater peace and core happiness**: Tremendous peace will come to you as you forgive yourself and others. This peace will demonstrate itself in many ways. You will sleep better, feel less depression, cope better and be less sensitive to others around you. You will learn more about yourself and who you really are. This will lead to feeling happiness from the inside out, something I call 'core' happiness.

》 **Relief from emotional pain associated with the past**: In a later section we will spend more time on overcoming the past; forgiving is a crucial step in doing that. You can relieve emotional pain associated with past events through authentic forgiving.

- **Selective remembrance**: This benefit is one of my favorites. One of the reasons we remember things that have hurt us is because of emotional imprinting. When we are hurt or offended, it creates an emotional event in our minds that is associated with the real event. This emotional imprinting causes pain each time we think of the event. As we remember and experience the associated pain again and again, the emotional imprint becomes reinforced. One way to reduce the effect of emotional imprinting is to forgive. I have personally experienced, and my clients have experienced a 'loss of memory,' if you will, once they have authentically forgiven themselves or their offender. This 'loss of memory' is an erasure of the emotional imprint; you no longer feel the pain. Sometimes you even forget the event itself! Imagine how that can free you to think on things that give you joy and peace instead!

- **Divine blindness**: After authentic forgiving you will see yourself or your offender in a different light. They won't be such an enemy to you. Not that you need to become their best friend, but you will see them in their innocence instead of their guilt. In effect, you become blinded to their guilt; I call it divine blindness. Seeing someone's innocence does not take them off the hook; they are still accountable. But with divine blindness, you approach it with less emotion and more objectivity.

- **Greater immunity to temptation:** This is a powerful benefit of forgiving. I cover this in depth with my religious clients. When you become a forgiving person who practices daily forgiving of yourself and others, you increase your ability to live with integrity. You develop greater strength to overcome your weakness and resist temptations. I have witnessed a recovering heroin addict reduce his cravings by practicing forgiving. Whatever your vice, you can gain more self-control through forgiving.

) **Acceptance of your own and others' weaknesses with greater ease:** As you practice forgiving and become a more forgiving person, it enables you to more comfortably accept your own weaknesses and the weaknesses of others. This is a result of learning to see yourself and others more in terms of innocence than guilt. When you see someone as guilty, almost anything they do or say will support your perception. The same is true if you see them in their innocence. We all see what we want to see.

) **Improved health:** As studies have shown, active forgiving has long term health benefits. Daily forgiving strengthens your immune system, which increases your ability to heal and respond better to needed medicinal or naturopathic treatment.

) **Relief of depression:** Depression is often a result of persistent negative thoughts. A lack of a forgiving attitude creates negative thinking and can damage your self-worth. Forgiving is like turning on a light in a dark room. It will illuminate the positive and eliminate the negative. In a study reported in the *Journal of Consulting and Clinical Psychology*, researchers found that forgiveness therapy did more to reduce the effects of depression than teaching them anger management or other interpersonal skills.[10]

) **Better relationships with EVERYONE:** Studies show that a propensity to forgive increases both the satisfaction and status of your relationships.[11]

) More and more studies demonstrate that forgiving has benefits beyond improved relationships. Teaching principles of forgiving has become a key professional tool in rehabilitating inmates; addiction recovery; addressing anxiety, depression and other mental illnesses. Don't disregard the benefits of forgiving, the way that 66% of Americans ignore the benefits of flossing until it is too late. Becoming an authentically forgiving person will do more for your health and well-being than almost anything else you do. Let me save you a lot of time, money and heartache. Forgive! Experience the miracles of forgiving.

I AM STRONG!

Chapter 17

Authentic Forgiving in Six Steps

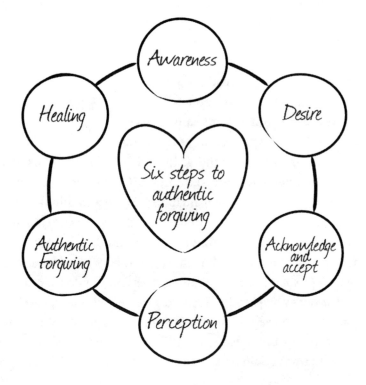

A uthentic forgiving is forgiving in the right way for the right reasons. It includes six important steps: awareness of the effects of withholding forgiveness and the need to forgive; inward sincere desire to forgive; acknowledgment and acceptance of the offense and the pain or injury it has caused you, as well as your responsibility to heal yourself or let God heal you; learning to see your offender differently; authentic forgiving; and healing, letting go and embracing freedom, compassion and joy.

Step 1: Awareness

Self-examination to create awareness of how not forgiving is affecting your life is a necessary step toward authentic forgiving. Examine with some objectivity the negative emotions you experience regularly. Are they associated with another person and how they have treated you? Do these negative emotions include emotional pain, anger, feelings of revenge or distrust? Do you blame someone for these negative emotions?

Carrey came to me complaining about her husband. She explained in some detail how hurt she felt by all the things he did or didn't do. She hated the way he treated her and expressed that 90% of her negative emotions were directly attributed to her husband. She wanted him to stop, to change, in order to make it all better. In other words, she wanted me to 'fix' him for her. I understood her desire and her need to feel relief from the pain and the hurt. The reality was that neither she nor I could change her husband; he is the only one that could do that. But it was within Carrey's power to forgive and give herself more peace. It took some time. Once she realized that by not forgiving she was adding to her own pain, she became open to the steps necessary to authentically forgive so that she could receive the benefits and miracles of forgiving.

I AM STRONG!

Remember that emotional pain, especially as it relates to the actions of others, is an indicator to take action to become better, rather than bitter. This action may include withdrawing from the source of the pain; identifying those things that require acceptance; stopping anything you are doing to contribute to the problem; or making appropriate changes in your circumstances or behavior. Taking action will also include forgiving. Awareness is an important step in recognizing what is keeping you from authentically forgiving. There are two types of barriers to authentic forgiving: outward and inward. Let me explain both.

Outward Barriers

Seeking vengeance: Wanting to get even and to fight back are very natural responses to being hurt, betrayed, stilted, embarrassed or set up for failure. We don't even have to be the victim to experience this tendency. We can get angry and seek revenge when it is a friend or family member who is the victim. Even if you are not the victim, you need to forgive. Vengeance can seem justified, but it is an indicator that you are out of peace and need to forgive in order to restore you to a peaceful state.

When retaliation is justified, it can be a very tempting option. You may consider yourself weak or wimpy for not fighting back. But there are many ways to stick up for yourself without resorting to retaliation. This past summer my wife and I were vacationing in Lake Tahoe, California, where we watched a news interview with the parents of a young teenage boy. Their son had been shot in a neighborhood park less than 24 hours before. I was impressed by this couple as they shared a message of hope and forgiveness. They expressed no ill will but a desire that whoever shot their son would turn himself in and get the help he needed. They could have easily justified retaliation but instead chose forgiveness and mercy.

Pride: Your own pride is another barrier to forgiving. Pride is an attempt to relieve emotional pain from being offended by assuming superiority over the offender or refusing to acknowledge your own weaknesses or imperfections. When we refuse to forgive, we are acting out of pride. In essence, we choose to be miserable over forgiving. I don't live in a fairy tale where everyone loves each other, nor am I so naive to think that these things are super easy. Pride is often a very natural response and, in some cases, an emotional defense mechanism. However, if persisted in, pride will keep you from healing, from feeling calm, peaceful, happy and content. It is worth acknowledging your own pride and considering humbling yourself to forgive those who have offended you.

Inward Barriers

Inability or unwillingness to forgive yourself: There is no social injustice in forgiving yourself. It is an act of self love, and for this reason, I have purposefully put the topic of forgiving after the topic of self-worth. If you find it hard to forgive yourself, I suggest you work on increasing your self-worth and understanding the great value you bring to the world and the people around you. You are worthy of your own forgiveness. You owe it to yourself to be forgiven. You are not being too easy on yourself if you forgive yourself. Remember, it doesn't mean you are a slacker or a wimp, it means you are prioritizing happiness over misery, although it certainly does not mean you are any less responsible or accountable.

Displacement: Withholding forgiveness does not happen without a price. It will affect you in other aspects of your life. One of the most common effects is anger, but not necessarily toward the person who has offended you. We often lash out at those closest to us because we are unwilling or feel unable to forgive ourselves or our offenders. Displaced anger is not fair to those around you, especially those closest to you, when your inability to forgive hurts them. Do yourself a favor and start the process of forgiving now to spare your loved ones the negativity, abuse, anger and emotional distress that you carry around.

Conflict in loyalty: Let's say your sister is devastated to learn that her husband has been cheating. You feel you should forgive your brother-in-law for all the reasons we have covered in this section, but to forgive him will appear to be disloyal to your sister. Forgive anyway. It may put you uncomfortably in the middle of a family controversy; but because it is the right thing to do, you will be a much better help to your sister if you can be objective and at peace. It does not mean you have to like or defend him. It does not mean that you condone his actions. It means that you will let go of hateful feelings and be at peace with yourself. Your peacefulness will help your sister forgive so she can return to peace as well.

Applying Step 1 –

Awareness: It is critical to become aware that you need to forgive, that not forgiving is causing you negativity, and that you may be creating internal and external barriers to forgiving.

- Start to look at feelings of revenge and desires to get even as indicators of your need to forgive. Visualize those feelings as a trigger to forgive, rather than a trigger to retaliate.

- Consider that you deserve your own forgiveness more than anyone else.

- Do the right thing. Forgiving is always the right thing. If something is keeping you from forgiving, then that is a signal to continue to work at it.

- Anger can be displaced as a result of not forgiving. Be honest about your anger; is an innocent person is being hurt because you are unwilling to forgive your offender?

Step 2: Desire

The desire to forgive must be born from within to be authentic. You may feel a lot of pressure from those around you to forgive. Perhaps you feel an obligation to forgive your trespassers in order for God to forgive you. As a young man I learned, "A man convinced against his will is of the same still." It applies

to you as well. Forgiving is an inside job and a decision you must come to on your own. The decision may not necessarily be about forgiving, as much as it should be about ridding yourself of emotional pain and distress. It is important to remember that forgiving is a means to an end, not the end itself. The end is your personal happiness and emotional freedom.

Jamie is allergic to poultry. This is not a common allergy; but if she eats any food that has been in contact with or has ingredients from chicken or turkey, it could be deadly. Once she purchased a package of sliced ham from the store, and after one bite she felt her throat swelling. She was having an allergic reaction. If she is not aware of what she is eating and aware enough to carry the right medication at all times, she could inadvertently consume poultry, causing an allergic reaction that could kill her. For Jamie, awareness is a life or death issue. Imagine having to be so aware of what you eat. We should be as careful and cognizant about our own emotional well-being. Think of negative emotions as an allergic reaction that causes you to swell up and itch if not remedied quickly. Your new allergy is an unwillingness to forgive. Your desire to be emotionally free should be as powerful as Jamie's desire to be poultry-free.

One way to create a desire to forgive is to visualize yourself forgiving those who have hurt or betrayed you. Visualization is a powerful skill. Here is how it is done: In your mind create a mental movie of you forgiving that person. Remember, that it does not necessarily have to include a face-to-face confrontation, but it should include some verbalization that you forgive them. Your mental movie should be as realistic and vivid as possible. Once you have created the mental movie, replay it several times until it becomes comfortable. Then add into the experience as many of the five senses (sight, sound, smell, taste and touch) as you can. This will make it more real. The most important aspect of this mental movie is how you feel before, during and after forgiving. Imagine yourself overcoming the barriers discussed in Step 1 of Authentic Forgiving. Include a visualization of how good you feel by forgiving. In your mental movie include the love, calmness and peace you feel shedding the burdens you have been carrying. In other words, visualize the rewards of forgiving.

This trains your mind and body to 'believe' in forgiving. The exercise will help you create the desire to forgive. The desire will actually grow within you. It will come from the inside out for all the right reasons. We want to develop the desire to love and do away with the desire to hate; to be at peace, rather than in distress; to be whole instead of incomplete.

Applying Step 2 –

Desire: Remember that the desire to authentically forgive is born from within. To create that desire, we must start from the inside out.

> ❯ Visualize yourself forgiving your offender. Imagine a vivid movie in your mind, where you are the star and you actually forgive yourself or the person who has offended you.

> ❯ Start to believe in forgiving as a means of achieving emotional freedom from the pain you are feeling.

> ❯ Think of not forgiving as a splinter; unless you extract it, the splinter will fester and could infect your entire body.

Step 3: Acknowledgement and Acceptance

For many years I felt that I was fine with my mother having abandoned me. I thought that I had dealt with it quite well. In actuality, I had buried those feelings and was unwilling to acknowledge how much it was affecting other aspects of my life. In this step, you are to acknowledge the hurt and how it has affected you and your life. Recall the actual offense or act that hurt you; un-bury it. Move beyond denial.

You may actually need to give yourself permission to hurt, to accept that the event happened and look forward to being done with it once and for all. This allows you to get out of the 'should haves,' the 'could haves,' the 'must haves,' to what it really *is*. Once you can acknowledge that you are hurt and that there needs to be a change in your own emotional well-being, you can then accept it. Don't worry too much about how to effect the change in your emotional well-being. That will come in the last step of healing. In this step, simply acknowledge it completely, and then choose to accept that what's done is done. Acceptance does not minimize what was done nor its effects on you and your life. Acceptance helps you redirect your energy and emotion away from nursing wounds too long and holding onto grudges and pain, to improving your happiness and satisfaction.

I would also ask you to acknowledge that forgiving your offender may be contrary to justice. It may contradict how others are telling you to respond, and it may oppose your sense of fairness. Yet, even if you were to receive perfect justice—you would still have to go through the process of forgiving in order to heal and be at peace. Forgiving is about you. Is it fair that you continue to suffer? Remember, as we discussed earlier, forgiving does not let someone off the hook unless you want to let them off the hook. They are still accountable for their actions. Forgiving is your way of taking *you* off the hook by prioritizing your own peace over seeing to it that you get fairness.

It is a natural response to want to lash out and defend yourself when you have been wronged, but it is in your best interest and well-being to act purposely, rather than over-react or react by default. When you are wronged you have a choice, and it is your choice alone; you can choose to become better or you can chose to become bitter. No one can 'make' you feel a certain way. It is your reaction to what has happened that causes those emotions. When you are wronged, acknowledged that you feel hurt, angry, sad, embarrassed, upset, betrayed. Then own those feelings.

Acknowledgment and acceptance is about helping you to stop blaming someone else for your misery. After we have been mistreated, it is so easy and natural to fall into the role of a victim. Sometimes it's valid to acknowledge that you've been a victim; we don't want to be dishonest and pretend nothing happened if something did happen to us. If we had not been wronged in some way, we would not even need to discuss forgiving. You cannot live life and not feel wronged at one time or another; but allowing yourself to remain a victim doesn't un-wrong the wrong that's been done to you. Acknowledge and take responsibility for your own emotions, thoughts, feelings, actions and words. You may have been victimized, indeed; but you don't have to *be* a victim—not when you can choose instead to be a survivor.

The power of acceptance has made a huge difference in my own life and in the lives of many of my clients. Claudia was having a tough time after her husband asked for a divorce. They had been married 22 years, and she just could not understand it. As much as she racked her brain, analyzed the past 22 years, spent time looking deep into her heart and searching for clues for what she could have done differently, she still could not figure out why her husband wanted a divorce. And she didn't believe his reasons why. Claudia was miserable and on the point of a breakdown. Some relief came when she finally accepted that she may never really know why her husband was making this choice. This is like the mom who asks her 12-year-old son why he teases his younger sister. The mom can ask all she wants, but there is no way for a 12-year-old to know why he does anything, let alone have the ability to articulate it well. Believe it or not, the same is true with most of us. It takes a lot of self-awareness to really know why we act a certain way in certain situations.

The same is true for your offender. They may not know, and you certainly will likely never know, the real reasons why. So it is time to just accept that and move on. Learn to be comfortable with not knowing. Many people condition their willingness to forgive upon understanding why. They say things like, "If I could just understand why they did it, I could forgive and get over it." If you are waiting to understand the reasons why, you will likely be waiting a long time. So accept that you may not ever know and move on.

Applying Step 3 –

Acknowledgment and Acceptance: There may be pain associated with acknowledging that you are hurt and owning your feelings. However, the pain of acknowledging hurt and accepting it will be shorter-term than the pain that comes with not forgiving.

Don't let the pain of the offense get the best of you. You don't have to live this way any longer. Accept that you are in pain, and take steps to rid yourself of it.

Realize that you may never know the real reasons why someone has offended you. You don't need to know in order to forgive.

Recognize that you only have the power to control your own emotions and feelings. You cannot compel someone to say they are sorry. Don't wait for an apology – forgive now!

I AM STRONG!

Step 4: Perception –
Seeing your Offender Differently

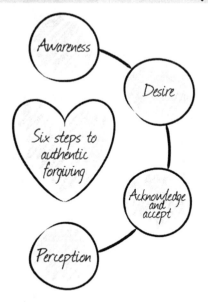

Whoever has offended you is now your enemy. In some cases you may think that it harsh to call your offender your enemy, but it is true. They may actually be a friend, a sibling, parent, co-worker or spouse, but if you harbor bad feelings toward them, you are actually seeing them as an enemy. You will soon resent them. This resentment is so powerful that it actually changes your perception, how you see them. Resentment demands to be justified, and so it will cause you to find all sorts of evidence to justify your animosity. Once we are offended, we find all kinds of reasons why our offender is a jerk. As long as we see them as our enemy, we are in defense mode. We watch what we say; we avoid them either physically or emotionally. We become guarded around them and feel like we need to be on our toes whenever they are around. This is tiring and destructive. If you are harboring bad feelings toward your spouse, you are seeing your spouse in a light that reveals all their weaknesses and flaws. Now, not only your spouse's offenses, but add to that your ill-perception of your spouse, is affecting your emotional well-being and your relationship. How can you feel emotionally close to someone whom you consider your enemy? That conflict alone will create negativity, robbing you of peace, happiness and satisfaction.

To authentically forgive, we need to embrace the enemy. By embracing them I don't necessarily mean to stop what you're doing and give them a hug, but to embrace who they are by trying to see them as they see us, and to see them as they see themselves. I often tell of having to experience emotional abuse from my stepmother. As a teenage boy, it was a horrible feeling to be ridiculed and put down constantly. Part of me knew I was a good kid (that is where self-worth comes in), and yet my self-image was constantly challenged by the way I was treated. In a miraculous experience I learned that if she really knew me, if my stepmother took the time to really see me and come to know me for who I was, she would not treat me that way. That allowed me to see her in her innocence (her inability to know me) – rather than in her guilt (how she was treating me.) That simple change in my perspective changed everything for me, and it can do the same for you. People who treat you poorly, put you down, criticize you, betray you, and beat you down don't really know you. If they did, if they knew how special you are, how wonderful you are, how capable you are, how smart and sincere you are, they would not treat you that way. At some point you just have to look at them and accept that they can't or never will know you and forgive them for that. In essence, without making excuses for them, you need to try and see them in their innocence instead of their guilt.

Just over a year ago, Debbie witnessed a dot get hit by a truck in front of her. She immediately pulled over and ran to rescue the dog. As she approached the wounded animal, the dog attacked her, severely injuring her with lacerations on her thighs and buttocks. As witnesses looked on, the dog attacked her again, this time biting off one of her fingers. I visited with Debbie a few weeks after the attack. I could tell she was still in pain and was trying to be extremely careful not to bump the stub of a finger on her right hand. However, Debbie was suffering more from the fact that several people stood by, including the driver of the truck, and did nothing to help her. She was filled with anger toward him and the others. I asked if she was angry toward the dog, and she said, "Not at all. That poor dog was wounded and only did what came naturally." In her mind, Debbie saw the dog as innocent, as reacting in self-protection and fear. She now had a choice. She could harbor negative feelings toward the witnesses that didn't help her, or she could see them the same way she saw the wounded animal —as wounded, innocent and reacting in self-protection and fear. As you can imagine, this traumatic experience will stay with Debbie for the rest of her life. She can choose to remember the event as unfortunate and get past it, or she can remember the event with anger and a need for justice.

The sooner that Debbie was able to see that the witnesses and the dog weren't that different, seeing them in their innocence instead of their guilt, the sooner she would be able to accept the situation, although unfortunate, and move on with her life. She stood to learn a great lesson about the power of choosing our perceptions, without forever carrying around the presently associated emotional pain.

Every action is done in love or as a cry for love. When you are able to see someone's misbehavior as a cry for love, you can see that they are wounded and need help. The help you can offer them is forgiveness. This is even more important for ourselves. You need to realize that the person you were when you made a past mistake is no longer the person you are now. Choose to look through a lens of compassion and concern and you will see that person differently—that is the person you forgive. When you can finally see your offender as someone trying to meet unmet needs or someone who is trying to protect himself, someone in need of your love, kindness and compassion, forgiving them is the next logical step.

Applying Step 4 –

Perception: Looking at someone differently can often be a difficult thing to do, especially when you are the one hurting.

> Giving your offender the benefit of the doubt does not let them off the hook. They are still accountable.

> Consider who might love your offender. Their mother? Their father? Try to see what they see.

> As an exercise, try to put yourself in the shoes of your offender. It may be difficult, but it might provide a basis for seeing them in their innocence instead of their guilt.

> Consider your offender a wounded animal – lashing out without really thinking about it.

> Change your mind about them. If you know them well, consider the positive things they have done previously, and dwell on those.

> Try to see your offender as not all bad and not all good, but somewhere in between.

Step 5: Authentic Forgiving

Notice that the steps to authentic forgiving do not start with forgiving. It is not until this step that you are adequately prepared to forgive. Without the proper and adequate preparation, forgiving can be a difficult and often unsuccessful. That is why I have spent so much time on steps 1-4, so that you can prepare yourself mentally and emotionally to forgive your offenders. In time, after practicing, you can quickly move through the first four steps. The act of authentic forgiving requires you to be in the right frame of mind. If you haven't let go of desires for revenge and still harbor ill feelings toward your offender,

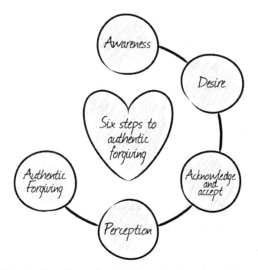

you may need to go back and spend more time on the previous steps.

The act of authentic forgiving is actually quite simple. Forgive in your mind first. This is why step 2 in the process is so important. As you visualized yourself forgiving, you have actually forgiven your offender in your mind already. Once you forgive your offender in your mind, then you can now verbalize forgiving. The person does not need to be present for this. You do this by saying out loud, "David, I forgive you and I release you." I recommend that you repeat this out loud several times. It may seem funny to actually forgive someone out loud without them there, but expressing forgiveness out loud makes it real. It gives authenticity and sincerity to the act of forgiving. After you repeat this several times, you should already notice relief from emotional pain and the emotional burdens you have been carrying.

My clients always ask me if they should meet face-to-face with their offender to forgive them. My response is always the same. I tell them, "You will know in your heart if you need to meet face-to-face to forgive them. But don't meet with them until you have already forgiven them in your heart." Forgiving them first in your mind, then out loud, allows you to release them from any emotional accountability before you actually meet with them. Otherwise the outcome is unpredictable, and you may not be satisfied with the meeting.

When it comes to authentically forgiving yourself, it is important that you truly forgive and then move on. You may still have to accept the consequences for your choices. But you have it within you to forgive yourself, learn from experience and choose better next time. One way to forgive yourself is to use these powerful words:

"Had I known better, I would have chosen better."

"Had I known it would hurt others as much as it did, I would have chosen differently."

And then follow with this statement, "I forgive myself and I release myself." These statements have been used with great success with many of my clients. I know that they will help you too. Don't feel limited to the words that I have included here. I would prefer that you use words that are personal and significant to you, as they will carry more meaning. These words are included here to help you get started. But almost immediately, you should start to feel different and ready for the last step, which is healing.

Applying Step 5 –

Authentically Forgiving: If you have taken steps 1 – 4 seriously, then the act of authentic forgiving is somewhat easier. In this step you forgive first in your mind and heart, and only then do you consider a face-to-face, voice-to-voice, email-to-email, text-to-text forgiving.

❯ Forgive in your mind and heart before you forgive in person, if you so choose.

❯ Forgive yourself first by having the new you, the person you are in this moment, forgive the *you of the past.*

❯ Forgive by getting used to the idea of forgiving. You do this by saying aloud, "David (if David is the person you are forgiving), I forgive you and I release you."

❯ Forgiving is something that should be done regularly and repeatedly until you feel the pain disappear.

I AM STRONG!

Step 6: Healing

Don't be discouraged if the emotional pain you have felt does not disappear immediately. Be patient and diligent. You may have to repeat the steps to get to the point of feeling of emotionally free of the pain you have felt for so long. It does work, and it makes a huge difference. However, this last step in the process should not be overlooked. It is important that you take care to actually heal because it is in the healing that we truly let go, rise above the offense and become stronger. Here are some tips to help the healing process:

Give yourself permission to forget. There are those of you who feel that you can never forget what someone has done to you. The

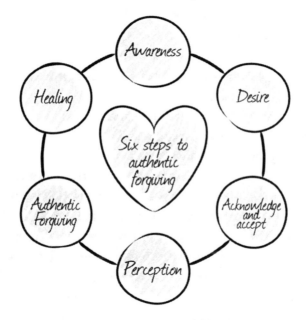

offense was so bad, too terrible to ever forget. To some degree I understand that you may want to hold on to the offense as a badge of courage. For example, I have mentioned my mother abandoning me several times in this book and in my previous book. It is an experience that has helped shape me into who I am today, the same way that your trials, adversity and pain have shaped you. I am not asking you to forget something that will make you better; I am suggesting something along the lines of selective forgetfulness. Allow yourself to forget aspects of the experience that cause you pain so you can grow, mature, develop and learn from the experience without the pain.

Recognize that it may take time to trust again. As previously mentioned, forgiving does not mean that you welcome your offender into full trust simply because you have forgiven them. Forgiveness and trust are separate things. You don't have to become best friends with those whom you forgive. For example, let's say that your partner stole money from the business, leaving you with extreme debt. After going through steps 1-5, you have now forgiven your partner. But it would probably not be wise to go into business with him again, particularly if you have not observed change sustained over time. As for a spouse who cheated on you, a son or daughter who stole from you, and so on, it may take time and wisdom to know if and when you should trust again. But if there is change demonstrated consistently over time, trust is easier to rebuild once you have authentically forgiven.

Rebuild safety. Often the situation and the circumstances surrounding an offense are significant to consider. For example, perhaps you were taken advantage of at a party after you had been drinking. One way to heal is to learn from the experience and curb your drinking so that you don't find yourself in that situation again. If your son or daughter or even their friends stole money or valuables from you, it is your right to set rules and boundaries on friends in the house and to even get a safe for your valuables. Perhaps you co-signed on a loan for a friend, and you were left with the payments. Part of healing is to learn from that and choose not to cosign for anyone else. How many times have you heard someone say, "Well, what doesn't kill you will only make you stronger"? I take exception to that saying because it is incomplete. The right way to look at this is to understand: that which doesn't kill us can make us stronger if we choose to become stronger. Part of healing after an offense is to learn from it.

Protect and preserve your self-worth. Although it was covered previously, I want to reinforce the concept here. Part of healing after forgiving is not to let what has happened to you or what you have done define who you are. What happens to you may knock your self-confidence down a notch or two, but it is not who you are. A divorce is something that happens to you; it is not who you are. Being cheated on is something that happened to you; it is not who you are. Being laid off or fired is what happened to you; it is not who you are. Protect and preserve your self-worth by separating what you do and what happens to you from who you are.

Surrender is another aspect of healing. Granted, there are some offenses that are too terrible to mention here, and I am sure some of you reading this may feel I have glossed over forgiving as it relates to really bad things. The principles I have shared with you here apply to the whole gamut of offenses, from little things that annoy you, all the way to abuse or losing a loved one to a violent act. Forgiving is a great gift that you give yourself to promote healing. If the offense is too great and too horrible, you may need to practice surrender by letting God take this over from you so that you can be at peace.

Applying Step 6 –

Healing: Healing is the most important step to authentic forgiving. Your forgiveness will be incomplete, and the pain may return unless you allow yourself to heal.

- ❯ Give yourself permission to forget by reminding yourself that the event and the pain is over whenever it comes to mind.

- ❯ Accept that trust may take time to rebuild. If you find it hard to be around your offender, accept that it may take time, and accept that you don't have to be best friends.

- ❯ Rebuild safety by making sure that the event, the situation, and the circumstances of the offense are not repeated.

- ❯ Surrender the pain, the experience, the burden to God or your higher power.

Beware of Inauthentic Forgiving

To be authentic, forgiving must be done in the right way for the right reasons. One of the countless examples of inauthentic forgiving is when you actually use forgiving as a tool of manipulation: to get someone to ultimately do what you want them to, to prove that you are superior, or to prove you are a good person, and so on. Manny and Carol, married for 23 years, felt they were at a standstill in their marriage. Both kept a long mental list of things the other person had done to hurt, disrespect, blame or embarrass the other. Manny would remind Carol of something on his list, followed by a variation of, "But I forgive you; I always forgive you." Manny was trying to demonstrate what a good person he was by always forgiving. He wanted to show his superiority over Carol by quickly forgiving; and then he wanted a pat on the back for it. Manny was falsely forgiving Carol. Not only was Manny forgiving in order to look like he was a good person, he was quick about it in order to stay in control, which is manipulation.

When you forgive for the wrong reasons, it will only lead to more emotional pain and regret. The regret turns into resentment that will destroy you and your relationships. Unfortunately, we have all experienced inauthentic forgiveness. For instance, if you feel pressured into prematurely forgiving someone in order to prevent the loss of their love or to keep someone from leaving, you are only prolonging the inevitable and may create a vicious cycle of repeated forgiving without healing. In contrast, you will know when forgiving is authentic because the emotional pain subsides and you become a new and stronger person.

In almost every coaching situation, I have found that focusing on authentic forgiving accelerates the healing process and leads to significantly more positive outcomes. You don't need to live with the burden of emotional pain any longer. The sooner you can trust the process of authentic forgiving and approach it with some seriousness, the sooner you will shed the skin of unhappiness you have been wearing. Like lizards, we too must shed on a regular basis. Let authentic forgiving become natural and frequent to the point that it becomes part of who you are. Self-worth and authentic forgiving are close cousins. The higher your self-worth, the easier it is to forgive others their trespasses against you; conversely, the more you become a forgiving person, the higher your self-worth. Authentic forgiving is one of those things in life that, once mastered, can truly change your life for the better and break down obstacles to your happiness and success. It takes both the courage and the strength you gain from practicing the I AM STRONG formula to authentically forgive.

Putting the Miracles of Forgiving into Action

Forgiving can be one of the most amazing and liberating experiences of your life. The six steps of authentic forgiving are not reserved for the big offenses only, but should be applied to anything that causes you pain as you remember an event or situation. Forgiving is a gift you give yourself, and it is all about you. The minute you think it is about the other person, you are putting your peace in jeopardy. Here are some suggestions to help you feel worthy of forgiving:

} Don't wait. The pain you are feeling is an indicator that you need to do something. Don't go another day without taking a step toward relieving that pain and restoring your peace.

} Beware of pride, as pride will do all it can to convince you that you don't need to forgive and cause you to demand that the other person apologize first.

} Remember that forgiving does not relieve someone from being accountable for making restitution or reconciliation.

} You don't have to be best friends with the person you forgive; rebuilding trust requires effort on the part of the person who broke your trust and it takes time. However, trust is easier to rebuild once you have forgiven.

} Forgive yourself first. You deserve your forgiveness more than anyone else.

} Trust in the six steps to authentic forgiving. They work; they will truly restore you to peace.

Personal Assessment on Forgiving

1	If someone offends me, I go out of my way to make them pay.
	Disagree 1 2 3 4 5 6 7 8 9 10 Agree
2	Forgiving doesn't seem to do any good.
	Disagree 1 2 3 4 5 6 7 8 9 10 Agree
3	I am willing to forgive once the offender has said he is sorry.
	Disagree 1 2 3 4 5 6 7 8 9 10 Agree
4	Forgiving just lets someone off the hook. They should pay for what they have done.
	Disagree 1 2 3 4 5 6 7 8 9 10 Agree
5	I may forgive, but I don't forget.
	Disagree 1 2 3 4 5 6 7 8 9 10 Agree
6	When I am offended, I hold a grudge for a long time.
	Disagree 1 2 3 4 5 6 7 8 9 10 Agree
7	I have done so much that is wrong, I find it hard to forgive myself.
	Disagree 1 2 3 4 5 6 7 8 9 10 Agree
8	I would rather get even than let someone get away with something.
	Disagree 1 2 3 4 5 6 7 8 9 10 Agree
9	If I forgive another who has hurt someone I love, I am letting my loved one down.
	Disagree 1 2 3 4 5 6 7 8 9 10 Agree
10	Forgiveness is embarrassing. It is a sign of weakness.
	Disagree 1 2 3 4 5 6 7 8 9 10 Agree
11	I find it very hard to confront others about what they did wrong against me.
	Disagree 1 2 3 4 5 6 7 8 9 10 Agree

12	I can't forgive until I am forgiven.										
	Disagree	1	2	3	4	5	6	7	8	9	10	Agree

13	Forgiving requires me to be a friend to someone who has hurt me. I don't think I can do that.
	Disagree 1 2 3 4 5 6 7 8 9 10 Agree

14	Forgiving lets someone off the hook so they are no longer accountable.
	Disagree 1 2 3 4 5 6 7 8 9 10 Agree

15	If I just wait long enough, time will heal the hurt I feel.
	Disagree 1 2 3 4 5 6 7 8 9 10 Agree

16	When I see someone who has offended me, I turn the other way and don't want to see them.
	Disagree 1 2 3 4 5 6 7 8 9 10 Agree

17	Forgiving is for religious people, and since I am not religious it is not for me.
	Disagree 1 2 3 4 5 6 7 8 9 10 Agree

18	I quickly forgive in order to avoid any confrontation.
	Disagree 1 2 3 4 5 6 7 8 9 10 Agree

19	I forgive because God wants me to.
	Disagree 1 2 3 4 5 6 7 8 9 10 Agree

20	Forgiving tells the offender that you agree with what they have done.
	Disagree 1 2 3 4 5 6 7 8 9 10 Agree

Add up the score from the 20 questions: _____

A score of 100 or more means you have a hard time with forgiving and should work on the topics in this section, as well as improving your self-worth.

A score of 99 or below indicates that that you have a healthy perspective on forgiveness. Make forgiving a habit!

I AM STRONG!

Part 4

From Victim to Hero in 90 Seconds

I AM STRONG!

Historical markers are found along almost every highway, not only in the United States, but also in other countries as well. We are all familiar with these signs or plaques that are placed along the highway that tell of something significant that happened in the area. The marker may tell the story of a historical event, such as a battle that was won or lost; a famous person; or a proximate tragedy. Personally, when I am on a road trip I am more interested in getting from point A to point B than stopping to read about what happened out in the middle of nowhere. Of course, there may be those of you who consider stopping at historical markers a memorable part of a road trip and look forward to learning more about the region you are driving through.

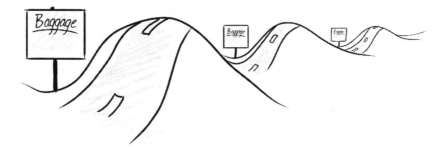

Like the highways we drive, the road of life is filled with ups and downs, high mountains, curvy roads and pleasant valleys. The mountains represent the hard times we have experienced, and the valleys represent when things were going well and we were content and happy. Along the road of life there are also historical markers – our own personal historical markers – events and experiences that have made an impact on us. Our historical markers are both positive and negative. Although we may not pay as much attention to our positive historical markers, we certainly don't want to ignore them. Most of us probably tend to remember and dwell on the negative markers. A historical marker for you might be something your father said that embarrassed you in front of your friends. It could be how your ex-husband treated you, or it could be that you were abused. These events, these experiences, these historical markers can come with intense emotion and pain. The next several chapters will focus primarily on those events and experiences that haunt you from your past and continue to cause you emotional pain or distress and rob you of peace.

Let me clarify what I mean about the past. When I refer to the past, you may instantly think of several experiences years ago that caused or still cause you the most pain. For the purpose of this section, the past includes anything that has happened before this very moment. It could be something that happened 40 years ago or 40 seconds ago. The past could even be something that you are currently experiencing or is ongoing. Regardless of the distance in time, too often, the past can ruin our day. When you are so focused on what has happened to you and identify yourself with it, whether it was a call to your cell phone company or being unfairly laid off, you don't have to let it ruin your day, or worse, ruin your life! You can overcome the immediate past, the recent past and the distant past. There is a lot of contemporary literature encouraging you to live in the moment, to be present. I agree with that, but sometimes the past has such a grasp on us that it creeps into the present and steals it away. Burying the past, ignoring the past is if it never happened, or letting time heal the wounds of the past are never effective. I propose a purposeful, proactive, and effective means of dealing with your past so you can indeed be present and live in the moment.

The skills I will share with you in this section will help you effectively overcome your negative past. These skills are equally effective with your distant and immediate past. Apply these skills to big things and small things. To start, let's consider your historical markers! Can you name them? Your historical markers are likely at the top of your mind. They are contained in the stories you tell yourself and others.

Practical Tip:

It will be helpful for you to list a few of your historical markers here by filling in the blanks below. For example, Jody might share a historical marker in this way, "I feel embarrassed and hurt because my father never told me I was pretty when I was growing up." Fill in the blanks below as specifically as you can. This will help you focus the skills in this section for the most benefit.

> I feel _____(examples: sad, angry, frustrated, hurt, jealous, resentful, cheated, fearful...) because _____.

> I feel _____(examples: sad, angry, frustrated, hurt, jealous, resentful, cheated, fearful...) because _____.

> I feel _____(examples: sad, angry, frustrated, hurt, jealous, resentful, cheated, fearful...) because _____.

> I feel _____(examples: sad, angry, frustrated, hurt, jealous, resentful, cheated, fearful...) because _____.

Each statement is a reflection that you have allowed yourself to be a victim of the past. Beware of being a victim, either having a victim mentality or identifying yourself as a victim to your past, because it will not only destroy your personal power but also have a devastating impact on your self-worth. You have a victim mentality when you falsely indentify with 'damage' done to you, or falsely identify yourself by the bad things that have happened to you. A victim mentality

in the extreme is when you are without hope, have an overwhelming sense of defeat and feel unable to exercise your free will. I would
not say you have a victim mentality if you feel temporarily defeated
and it takes some time to get your feet back under you. But dwelling
on the past, associating your identity with past events, neglecting to
believe in yourself or believe that your actions can make a positive
difference, and blaming others for your misfortune are good indicators that, to some degree, you victimize yourself. A victim mentality can contribute to your anxiety, depression and lack of motivation.
Already in this book I have covered two topics that can dramatically
help you overcome being a victim: investing in your self-worth and
authentic forgiving. We will use previous sections as a backdrop and
foundation to overcoming real events and experiences that cause you
emotional pain.

Chapter 18

You Have a Choice

It's not what happens to you that makes the difference; it is your reaction to what happens to you that matters. As with most things, you have a choice in how you react. With regard to past events and circumstances, your reaction includes not only your initial

Negative Past Event

CHOICE

Positive or constructive reaction

↓

Leads to:
Growth
Wisdom
Character
Experience

Negative or destructive reaction

↓

Leads to:
Baggage
Negative emotion
Burdens
Victim mentality

reaction in the past, but also your current reaction to the past as well. Our reactions, past and current, affect our life in the present and are reflected by the story we tell ourselves about what happened to us.

Take Abby for instance. Abby is now 38 years old and has been divorced for five years. You would only need to listen to Abby for a minute or two to understand how she feels about her divorce. She will readily share the pain, suffering and events leading up to, surrounding and after her divorce with anyone who will listen. Although it has been five years, Abby recounts the story of her divorce as if it were yesterday. I am pretty sure that the story she tells everyone else about what happened to her is the censored version of the story she tells herself. What are the stories you tell yourself about what happened to you? Are these stories of overcoming adversity and growing from it? Or are these stories, like Abby's, the ones where everything you are experiencing right now is judged by your past?

You have a choice; you can either react negatively to your past, causing the past to negatively affect your present circumstances and well-being; or you can react positively and grow from it. A negative or destructive reaction will most likely result in unwanted baggage, negative emotions, burdens and a victim mentality. Positive or constructive reactions almost always lead to growth, greater wisdom, better character and contentment. Most of us recognize this. On an intellectual level we understand that we have a choice on how to handle the past. However, seldom do we know how to actually make that choice.

Emotional Imprinting

Have you ever wondered why you remember some things and can't remember others? Why do we all remember little insignificant events when we did something stupid or stuck our foot in our mouth, and yet we have a hard time remembering to take out the trash, feed the cat or return a rented vide? Why we remember some things and quickly forget others is something of a mystery to me. However, part of the reason we remember past events, especially negative ones, is that it is not just a factual memory. In fact, it may not have much to do with the facts at all, but have more to do with how we felt in that moment. I call this emotional imprinting. This occurs when an event transpires in such a way that it leaves an emotional imprint on our mind. For example, a soldier suffering from post-traumatic stress disorder from time spent on the front lines in Iraq may intellectually know that firecrackers at an Independence Day celebration are not mortars and bombs, but the sound itself could cause him extreme and anxiety and discomfort. Why? Because of the powerful emotional imprint the event created.

Let me share with you another example from my own life. On October 1, 1987, a 5.9 earthquake hit Whittier, California, causing significant damage to many of the houses in our neighborhood. The quake hit at 7:42 a.m. at the moment my 6-year-old daughter, Meghan, had walked into the kitchen for breakfast. My wife was in the back of the house, and I was at work. The quake shook our house violently, causing the kitchen cupboards to throw dishes to the floor. The sound was deafening; and even though the duration of the quake itself was 20 seconds or less, it had a profound impact on our young daughter. For weeks after the quake, Meghan would not go into the kitchen. She wet the bed. She would barely leave our side. She did poorly in school and had a hard time sleeping. With the help of great counselors and friends, Meghan was able to resume her normal activities within six months.

It wasn't until a few months later that we realized that there might be some long-term effects. Meghan was afraid to ride in elevators. Even now, 23 years later, she has a hard time in elevators. The quake shook the house for less than 30 seconds, and yet the effects are still felt more than 23 years later. Why? Because of the emotional imprint it left on her mind. Meghan knows on an intellectual level that she is probably safe in an elevator, but it causes her anxiety, nevertheless. What are the earthquakes that have happened in your life? What are those events that, although you can put them in perspective on an intellectual level, have left an indelible imprint emotionally?

Emotional imprinting can also cause incorrect pattern matching. I will tell you a real life situation to make my point. Deb fell head over heels in love with Dwayne. He was charismatic, charming and attentive. Deb found in Dwayne everything she wanted in a man and felt that he was certainly going to propose, to which she would most definitely say yes. Dwayne had a great job, was physically fit, tall and handsome. Of the few vices in his life, Dwayne cherished and took very good care of his red Porsche 911. Things were going amazingly well between Deb and Dwayne. She was more than madly in love; she was totally and completely in love with Dwayne.

Two years after meeting Dwayne, Deb was fully expecting to be engaged at an upcoming dinner with Dwayne's family. The dinner didn't happen. Dwayne stood her up for the dinner and later texted her to say that it was over between them. Deb later learned that Dwayne had been cheating on Deb the entire time they were together! It has been several years since, and to this day, Deb will not date any man that drives a red sports car. Unfortunately, Deb has incorrectly matched red sports cars with jerks and is unable to get past it. Past events in our lives that cause an intense emotional imprint can cause us to make incorrect associations. Deb's true love might indeed drive a red sports car, but she is unavailable to anyone who owns one. Dwayne's rejection had nothing to do with the car he drove, but we all judge our present based on the filters created by our past experiences. If you ever needed a definition of emotional baggage, this would be it.

Practical Tip:

Take a moment to reflect and then write down some of the emotional imprints you may have. These could even be related to the historical markers you wrote down in the previous practical tip.

I AM STRONG!

Learned Helplessness

Another way that the past can indeed impact us in the present is something known as learned helplessness. Learned helplessness was a term first introduced by Dr. Martin Seligman, based on experiments with dogs in the late 1960s. Dr. Seligman demonstrated that dogs that were subjected to electrical shock with no apparent way of controlling the shocks learned to give up. They learned to be helpless.[12]

This can also be observed in people.[13] For instance, some people who have failed at tasks in the past can mistakenly conclude that they are failures and that nothing they do will make a difference. By their experience they have learned to be helpless. I am sure you have seen this in children and adolescents, and perhaps even adults. My own observation is that learned helplessness can become a powerful excuse that provides self-justification for failure. For some it is a defense mechanism, while for others, they believe it is who they are. Imagine growing up where all you heard from your parents, those who are supposed to be your biggest fans, supporters, and protectors was that you are stupid and can't do anything right. You will have a hard time being persistent to accomplish something you have previously failed at.

You can also learn helplessness through observation. If you struggle with your weight and have witnessed one or more of your parents fail at diet after diet, you may have learned that there is nothing you can do, so you might was well just live with being overweight. It is unfortunate that well-intending parents likely provided you with the very training you are now struggling to overcome. The problem is that you believed you are helpless; you need to shake free of that belief. You are not helpless. Your actions do make a difference. You can do hard things! What makes one person persevere and another give up? It could very well be what they have been taught. Were you taught to take personal risks or were you taught to be helpless?

Narrow Self-Labeling

The past is what we know. The present is unpredictable, and the future is a mystery. Because we are so familiar with our past, we can easily construct an identity based on what happened to us. The emotional imprint of one negative experience can be so powerful that we generalize it to the point of defining ourselves based on one or just a few negative experiences. Jonathan had not been that lucky in love and was determined not to get into another relationship like his last one. In his last relationship, everything was going well until he met her parents. They liked him but were concerned about his religious views. Jonathan was spiritually inclined but had chosen not to attend a specific church. His girlfriend, Lana, was the same way, and it seemed that together they were compatible and made a good couple. But the religious pressure from her parents was too much, and so Lana dumped Jonathan. A few months later Jonathan fell in love. He didn't mean to, but it was love at first sight. The next several months were wonderful as they got to know one another. However, when they started talking about raising children, it was clear that once again, religion would be a deal breaker. Jonathan wanted a more open approach to religion, and his new love was set on raising children within her church. Jonathan broke it off and couldn't understand why this 'always' happened to him. "Why," he asked, "do I always attract girls who can't accept me for who I am? Why do I always pick the wrong girls?" Although this did indeed happen to Jonathan twice, it does not mean that it 'always' happens to him. He was labeling himself too narrowly. He was taking a few specific events in his past and spreading it like lard across his whole life. Jonathan was taking specific events, over-exaggerating them and generalizing them to include his future and every experience.

Have you done this? Do you label yourself based on your past negative experiences? Are you a divorcee or are you a woman who got a divorce? Do you call yourself a total failure, even though you have not failed at everything? I often speak to people who think that they are irrevocably damaged because of what has happened to them in the past. I once had an employee that referred to herself as stupid, incompetent and weak. She berated herself for not being able to stick up for herself and be mature. By getting to know her better I was able to understand that there were a few things in her past that could be best described as errors in judgment and moments of weakness. The problem is that she was basing her whole identity on a few bad choices; she had labeled herself so narrowly that in her own mind there was no room for change. No matter what has happened to you, you are not damaged goods. You are not a failure simply because you have failed at a few things. At the end of this section, I will share how to redefine failure as success. You are more than what has happened to you. Try to balance out your perspective of the past by recalling and dwelling on positive events and using that as your label.

Having a Love Affair with the Past

There is nothing wrong with some level of romanticizing the past and remembering the great experiences. There is some great benefit in a balanced nostalgia that allows you to savor past accomplishments and happiness. Looking back over the past as a means of measuring progress is a healthy thing to do as well. However, putting too much emphasis on the past and romanticizing it to the point of disregarding the present is unhealthy. Most cars I have driven have at least one rear-view mirror. They are essential to safe driving. Would you ever consider driving by only looking in the rear-view mirror? It sounds absurd, but I have met many great and wonderful people who do just that in their lives. They glorify the past to the point that they contrast every experience in the present to it. They use the past to highlight what is so bad about today, and they don't limit their judgment to politics, healthcare and the economy. They will use it to judge people, places, things and new experiences. To them, nothing is as good as the good ol' days.

A few years ago my wife and I took a walking tour of the German walled city Rothenburg o der tauber. This is one of the few cities in

Germany with an intact wall around the city. During our walking tour, the guide stopped for a minute to make a point about romanticizing the past. He said, "Whenever I give this tour describing the life in this city, someone always says, 'Those were the good ol' days!' Don't believe it," he said. "Life was hard, harder than it is today. It was dirty and smelly. You could be walking down the street and someone from above would dump their sewage on you. There was no indoor plumbing, and they had to get rid of it somehow, so they just threw it out the window!" We remember what we want to, and it is based on a variety of factors such as emotions, attitudes, feelings and circumstances. Seeing the past as only positive and idealized is a biased view that leads you to believe that the present doesn't have anything to offer.

Another result of being too nostalgic is that it can create fear of the future. People who dwell on the past in all its glory create a restrictive comfort zone around them that causes anxiety over trying something new. They become fearful of change. If the change is too drastic, they long for a return of the past, unable to live in the moment and embrace the present. The past is never as bad, nor as good, as you think. Create a balanced view of the past that allows you to learn from past mistakes, savor the good and happiness of the past without biasing the time you are living in right now.

Chapter 19

Don't Let the Past Ruin Your Day!

We are not separate from our past. The past and the present are connected. There are many of you who would like a 'do over' when it comes to your past or would like to remove the historical markers from the road of your life. The past is what it is, and you can try to pretend that it isn't, or you may have gone to great efforts to bury or hide your past; but as hard as you may try, your past is manifesting itself in your present. A cat climbs up on a stove to take a seat, only to learn that the stove was hot. It is logical to assume that the cat will never do that again. But is the cat smart enough to not sit on a hot stove or not to sit on any stove? It is unfortunate, but if that were to happen to us, we too might avoid all stoves, hot or cold, thinking we will get burned. How is your past manifesting itself in your present world?

Pity Parties: When the past is repeated in the present, it is hard not to feel sorry for yourself, and there is nothing wrong with calling a friend or two for consolation. However, when this becomes you modus operandi for everything in your life and you start to need, crave or demand attention in the form of people feeling sorry for you, then it has gone too far. When you victimize yourself to feel better or to get attention, the past that you want to overcome or forget starts to play a greater role in the present than it should. Feeling sorry for yourself won't do much good; it actually keeps you cycling through a rut. I refer to pity parties as "lingering in the valley of sorrow." Refuse to linger. You don't need to throw pity parties any longer. You can rise above your sorrows and feel great by unburdening the past and living fully in the present.

Lumping: When our present situation is negative, it is hard not to connect the dots between all the negative things that have happened in your past in an effort to make some sense of it all. When we connect the dots in that manner, it is like lumping all the bad things that have happened to us on top of one another. This not only ruins the present but also causes us to erroneously predict mostly negatives for the future. Lumping exaggerates your present, negative circumstance by piling on the past, making you want to give up because "this always happens to you." People who lump tend to think in worst-case-scenarios. Lumping prevents you from ever escaping your past because you carry it around, adding new bad experiences to your baggage.

Singled Out: Our bad experiences of the past can make us feel singled out in the present when we think that we are somehow strange, unworthy or damaged goods because of what has happened to us. I remember the first time my wife and I went to a marriage counselor, thinking that our marriage was doomed because of our problems. At first we were shocked to learn that our problems weren't unlike thousands of other couples. While that alone did not resolve our issues, it helped to know that we weren't unusual. There is a strange comfort in knowing that we don't suffer alone and that you are not the only one who has experienced bad things in your past. Whether you suffered emotional, physical, or even sexual abuse, or whether you have made mistakes that have caused others to suffer, you are not alone. There are others who have experienced the same things.

Doomsday Psychic: A doomsday psychic is someone who incorrectly predicts the future by creating mistaken certainties based on the past. For example, at the end of a job interview on Tuesday, the hiring manager told Brad that a decision would be made by Friday. When Friday came and went without a phone call, Brad become anxious and created in his mind all the reasons why he didn't get the job. Similarly, Shelia left a message for her boyfriend to call her back because she had something exciting to share with him. When he didn't call back right away, she started to freak out, imagining all sorts of reasons, from him cheating on her to wanting to break up with her. We have all done this, where our discomfort with unknown facts causes us to jump to wrong conclusions about others or make unfounded predictions about the future. The sky is not falling; the world is not coming to an end. It is better to just stick with the facts, stick with what you know. In both cases, Brad and Shelia had nothing worry about. Brad got the job, and Sheila's boyfriend's phone had lost its charge. Don't ruin the present by making up negative reasons why things don't happen the way you want them to within the time-table you expect.

Identity Theft: When you identify with your past to the point of defining yourself by your past problems, you have allowed the past to steal your identity. Shanna considered herself a divorcee, although she had been divorced for more than eight years. Everyone she met knew almost instantly that she was divorced and that it was a messy divorce. You see, in her mind Shanna was not a woman who got divorced eight years ago; she considered herself *a divorcee*. Similarly, Joanne was diagnosed with Type 2 diabetes three years ago. Instead of considering herself a woman with diabetes, in her mind she is a diabetic. You are not your body; you are not your net-worth or your diagnosis. When you construct your identity and define yourself based on your past, you rob the present of its beauty and the blessings you could enjoy this very moment. Part 1 on self-worth helps you define yourself based on who you are, not on what has happened to you.

Practical Tip:

In what way is your past manifesting itself in the present? Mark the one that best describes you:
- Do you throw personal pity parties?
- Do you lump bad past experiences onto present circumstances?
- Do you feel singled out because of your past?
- Are you a doomsday psychic, able to predict that bad will happen?
- Do you let the past identify who you are in the present?

I AM STRONG!

Chapter 20

From Victim to Hero
in 90 Seconds

This chapter is designed to help you learn five practical and powerful skills to overcome your past and free yourself from emotional burdens, baggage, pain and stress. In essence, you will learn how to avoid letting the past ruin your day. I realize that your past may include very serious and tragic experiences. In no way do I want to minimize the seriousness of any event in your past, nor do I want to make it any less important or significant. However, if the past is creeping into your present-day life, then it is time to make a change, a permanent change. Today is the day to no longer be a victim to your past, but to become a hero to your past. By hero, I don't mean that you are going to wear a cape and mask and fight crime; as a hero, you will be the opposite of a victim. You will be able to look at your past from a learning perspective. Instead of holding you back, your past will become the foundation for your success.

Over the years that I have taught this concept, I never cease to be amazed by the impact and freedom it brings to those who take this skill seriously and incorporate it into their lives. Why put up with being a victim for a minute longer? Once you learn how not to let the past ruin your day, it will take less than 90 seconds to go from being victim to hero. Let me now share with you five practical skills that will lift the pain, burden and negativity off your shoulders as you implement them.

1. Stay focused on today. You may have read books that counsel you to stay in the moment, to be present and avoid being distracted by the past or the future. This is sage advice but should not be taken to the extreme. For example, some homeless people are living in the moment and take little heed of the future. They are focused on their present situation, and although they are able, some "can't be bothered about the future." A better approach is to develop a healthy perspective on the past, so that it can provide a foundation of growth and learning with the appropriate anticipation, not fear, of the future. One way to experience this is to let today's problems be enough for today. This is the cure for lumping, as it was described previously. Don't lump your past onto your present. Let the past be a great teacher, helping you address present concerns; but don't generalize that "this always happens" to you or wonder why you should even try because it hasn't worked out in the past. We all have problems; you may be experiencing real tough problems and situations right this minute. Your problems are enough for today without lumping your past on top of it. Let today's problem be enough for today.

Practical Tip:

When you are tempted to lump other problems on top of one another, simply say to yourself, "Today's problems are enough for today."

---

2. Redefine failure as success. Are you a popcorn lover? If so, you know that one of the best known brands of popcorn is Orville Redenbacher. Orville Redenbacher dedicated his life to his passion of creating the world's best popping corn. He made more than 10,000 attempts to create the lightest and fluffiest popcorn on the market.[14] If asked, Orville would never pity or lament the fact that he failed 10,000 times. He would say that he succeeded by learning what not to do. We need to take the same approach by looking at our past and sincerely asking, "What did I learn?" When you move from a position of knowing (what happened) to a position of curiosity (what did I learn), you actually change your mental perspective from looking at your past as a series of failures to a series of learning experiences.

From a very young age we have been taught the black-and-white of failure and success. Although we know intellectually that it would be more accurately described in terms of shades of grey, it's still easy to think that if an experience does not turn out the way we want or expect, then we have failed. That thinking must stop if you are to overcome your past and if you are to start truly enjoying your abundant self-worth.

Michael Jordan is considered one of the world's greatest basketball players. About his own apparent failures, he said, "I have missed more than 9,000 shots in my career. I have lost almost 300 games. On 26 occasions I have been entrusted to take the game's winning shot... and missed. I have failed over and over again in my life, and that is why I succeed."[15] You can apply this same thinking to your past. You are who you are because of the combination of your successes and your failures. There is much to be learned from losing. There is so much more to be learned from adversity, trials and mistakes than there is to be learned from smooth sailing in life. Use your failings and struggles to gain experience and learning, which is your foundation of success. Turn those stumbling blocks into stepping stones.

Let me share one more related story with you. In 2005 an elderly woman in South Korea known to many as Grandma Cha Sa-soon wanted a driver's license so she could use a vehicle to sell vegetables and goods. But she failed the written driver's test. So she took it again. And again. She took the driver's license test once a day, five days a week. After 2008 she reduced her attempts to twice a week, but she never quit. She kept taking the test at the cost of $5.00 for a bus trip that was more than 2 hours round trip. She finally passed the test on her 960th attempt. Did Grandma Cha Sa-Soon fail 959 times? NO! It took great sacrifice in both time and money, but she learned how to take the test from all of her practice and attempts at it. We, too, can have the same tenacity to accomplish our dreams. When we eliminate the word 'failure' from our vocabulary, we eliminate a great source of negativity from our life. We begin to see ourselves and our challenges differently. This especially applies to past experiences that you have felt were failures until now. Look at those experiences as stepping stones. They are an advantage, not a disadvantage.

As we discussed earlier, remember this more complete version of the old axiom: what doesn't kill you will only make you stronger – *if you choose to become stronger*. We have a choice: to become bitter or to become better. Bitterness begets pain and suffering, while the choice to become better yields peace. Although it's not how we'd like it to be, it is often that the worst experiences and the biggest jerks in our lives are our best teachers. The choice is one of growth: to grow from the past or shrink into a victim mentality. Learning to redefine failure as success helps you turn your disadvantages into advantages. Look at almost any successful person, and you will likely find that they had to overcome great adversity to be successful. Whether it was overcoming poverty, abuse, a learning disability, or fear, most successful people have taken what may seem like a disadvantage and made something of it. They learned from it instead of letting it hold them back.

Practical Tip:

Whenever you think about a past mistake, trial, adversity, or a time when things did not turn out the way you expected, ask yourself this question with real intent: "What did I learn from that? How did I grow from what happened?"

---

3. Balance worst case scenarios with best case scenarios. Andrea is gifted. I say this sarcastically, referring to her great talent of identifying the worst case scenario out of the tiniest of data. If a friend doesn't call her back, it was because of something Andrea had said. If someone was late to an appointment, it was because something terrible happened. Andrea was the best at worst case scenarios. For those of us who have lived through worst case scenarios, it is not that hard to look at any situation and predict a terrible outcome. When challenged we can simply say that we are being a realist or taking an objective point of view. In theory there is nothing wrong with a little bit of realism. In some aspects, it is important to look at things with scrutiny in order to decide the best option.

But let's face it; you're not going to get a terrible outcome 100% of the time. So why predict the worst case scenario 100% of the time? Or even 90% of the time? In every scenario there are at least two possible outcomes – a worst case and a best case. Reality is that the outcome will lie somewhere in between. Let go of your past by casting aside worst case predictions based on your past, and come up with a best case scenario. You will be surprised at the outcome. By discarding black and white predictions, you will become comfortable with the unknown. By learning to balance every worst case scenario by creating a best case scenario, you will begin to believe in best case scenarios.

Practical Tip:

Next time you even feel yourself drawn to imagine a worst case scenario, you don't need to stop; simply add a best case scenario to your thinking to balance it out.

4. Believe that everything happens for a reason. How often have you heard someone say "everything happens for a reason" when you were going through a rough time? Do you believe it? Perhaps you too use this statement to help others get through a bad experience. Perhaps you think it yourself to relieve your pain. I have used it, and

I believe it. I do believe that everything happens for a reason. However, I also believe that just saying 'everything happens for a reason' is incomplete. It is more accurate and complete to say, "Everything happens for a reason – but you get to choose the reason!" Yes, things do happen for a reason, and when you assign a reason that is personal, meaningful and significant to things that happen, you immediately change your trial or challenge into a blessing. Using this skill in conjunction with choosing to learn from your past keeps a present challenge from becoming a negative experience.

Giving meaning to your suffering is a powerful coping mechanism. I believe that we are all on a quest for significance. Unfortunately, our search for significance is riddled with upsets and obstacles that become our historical markers along our life's journey. You don't need to wait for some miraculous event to happen in order for you to find your meaning. You don't need to wait for years to pass before you understand why something happened to you. Feel the power of meaning and purpose by choosing to assign to your struggle a reason that is personal, meaningful and significant.

How did I come to discover this for myself? In December of 1986, I was diagnosed with cancer. Wanting to keep it secret, I told very few people, which only added to my suffering and bewilderment. After seven long years, I was declared cancer-free. It was a glorious time, and we celebrated as a family with our four children, then aged 3, 7, 10 and 12. We celebrated Daddy's new cancer-free status with banners on the garage and a nice dinner. It was a huge milestone for my family. Three months later as I was rolling over in bed, I felt a new lump in my abdomen. Sure enough, it was another tumor but from a different form of cancer. We were devastated. After meeting with the doctor and trying to come to grips with a dismal prognosis, we gathered our little family together in the living room. How does a 34-year-old father explain to his children that he has cancer again? All I could do was tell them the truth – that I had a new form of cancer, and at the moment the prognosis was unknown. My two oldest children took it quite well. My youngest really didn't know what was happening. My middle son, with a sad face and tears in his eyes, climbed up on my lap and hugged me. With his mouth next to my ear, he said, "Daddy, I don't want you to die!"

The next morning I was at the hospital early for my first round of chemotherapy. It did not go well. I quickly developed an infection and ended up in the hospital for 30 days. During that time I knew I was going to die. I was either going to die from cancer, chemotherapy, the infection, or just plain hospital boredom! I was sick, I was lonely, and I was worried. Knowing that 'everything happens for a reason' was no longer as comforting as it once had been. I racked my brain to discover what the reason for this could be. Then it hit me! Everything does happen for a reason, but you get to choose the reason! In that moment I chose a reason that was personal, significant and meaningful. For me, the reason for my cancer was so that I could share this experience with others and help them get through it. As soon as I chose a reason, the pain, the adversity, the fear all had meaning, and I found renewed strength to the degree that I told the nurses, "Bring it on! Give me double the chemo!" When you choose a reason for your suffering that is personal and significant, you change your experience to a meaningful experience. You can do this with any experience you have had or are having. Everything happens for a reason, but you get to choose the reason!

When I teach this skill, the question I get most often is, "What if I don't pick the right reason?" When we are dealing with something serious, it is normal to want to pick a reason that is fitting and applies to the situation. However, don't worry too much about whether it is the perfect and most appropriate reason. If it is the wrong reason, you will know, and you will know almost right away because you won't feel the relief you anticipated. Is the reason important? Yes! You want to ponder and think of an appropriate reason and select one that is aligned with your beliefs, morals and values. For instance, if you decided that the reason you were suffering was because you deserved to be punished by God or to be a martyr, I am not sure those are the best reasons to choose. Reasons that include personal growth, self-examination, learning compassion, or being motivated to do something new are all good reasons to choose from. Pick a reason that is personal and aligns with truth, love, hope and your own internal value system, and you will feel that it is right almost immediately. It is also ok to change the reason as you grow and develop. This is particularly true when you are suffering from an ongoing difficult situation.

Does everything happen for a reason? I like to think so because the opposite is a terrible option. Victor E. Frankl was imprisoned during World War II and observed the power of finding meaning in suffering. He saw men and women die for no apparent physical condition or reason, other than that they had just given up. They had no meaning or reason to continue in the deplorable conditions of the Nazi concentration camps. Frankl is known as the father of Logotherapy – which can be summed as 'healing through meaning.' In his book *Man's Search for Meaning*, Frankl quotes the philosopher Nietzsche, "He who has a why to live can bear with almost any how".[16] It is as true today for you as it was for Frankl. When you have a reason to suffer, when you have a reason to go through the trials you are facing, that meaning alone can bring you solace, peace and strength. And while it may not resolve the problem, issue or challenge, it gives you courage to press on.

Practical Tip:

From now on when you are tempted to say, "Everything happens for a reason," complete the phrase by adding, "but you get to choose the reason!" You don't have to have a reason in mind the minute you say this, but the sooner you choose a reason, the sooner you will find hope, relief and strength. You may even want to write down your reason and your feelings about it.

5. Retell the story you tell yourself. Of all the skills in this section and perhaps even in this book, learning to retell the story you tell yourself about what happened to you in the past so that you are hero of that story and no longer the victim is probably the most powerful. Think of one of your historical markers that creates pain; now imagine that historical marker becoming a positive guidepost in your life. Doing this requires you to apply all of the previous skills in you've learned in this book, and doing so will dissolve your pain and relieve you of the burden you have been carrying. Our historical markers are re-lived in our minds every day when we tell ourselves the story about what happened. It is as if we have taken a pause from our journey on the road of life to re-live the event, as if we were standing in front of a historical marker reading it. Perhaps you have embellished and exaggerated the story so many times that you don't even remember the actual events. The stories we tell ourselves can be a coping mechanism, as we try to make sense of terrible events. Or maybe the events you are thinking of are so painful that to remember them in too much detail would be devastating. The way we tell our stories can be therapeutic, a healing way to deal with the past. Or it can be demeaning if we keep putting ourselves down for past mistakes and blunders.

Regardless of the story, regardless of the event, you don't have to let that event ruin your day. This is true whether the event happened 50 years ago, a year ago, a week ago or just this morning. Don't let the past ruin your day. Become the hero of your own story by learning how to retell it.

By example, let me continue the personal story I mentioned in the section on forgiving. It was the Friday before the new school year, and I was eight years old. My mother called my brother, sister and me and said, "Let's celebrate the end of summer and the starting of school on Monday." She gave us a list of things to buy at the store. She said we could spend the change on candy and eat it in the park on the way home. My siblings and I walked several blocks to the grocery store. We tried to be very frugal shoppers, hoping to minimize our expenses and maximize the left-over money for candy. I don't remember how much candy we bought, but we spent ample time in the park eating it. We then went home, anxious to see our mother and thank her for the candy. We got home, opened the door and discovered that the house was empty and mom was gone. It was not until I was 22 that I saw my mother again for a short visit. Between 22 and 48 years old, I only saw her a few times.

Now that I have told you this story, you can imagine possible negative emotional outcomes I may have experienced in my life because my mother abandoned me when I was eight years old. And the timing was terrible because my grandfather, with whom I was very close, had passed away just ten weeks earlier. For a moment go ahead and become an arm-chair counselor; I'm sure you can think up a litany of problems and issues that have probably plagued me throughout my life. What are some of the problems you think I would have to face? Trust issues? Especially trusting women? What about anger, lack of self-worth and self-confidence? How about low grades or learning disabilities? How about parenting issues or not being able to keep a job? Add on top of that the potential for drug use, alcohol abuse, infidelity and depression. Think about this: I could excuse myself with my story to the police, a friend, a counselor or a boss, explaining, "I have issues because my mother abandoned me," and they would probably sympathize and understand. It could be my universal excuse for almost any misbehavior. Fortunately, very few of those problems have been a resultant part of my life. I was blessed that it did not affect me as much as or in the ways that it could have. I am not exactly sure when it first happened or how it came about, but I feel grateful that from a very early age I was able to retell the story from an emotionally generous perspective, rather than seeing myself as a victim.

Before I explain further, let me ask, is there anything that an eight-year-old boy could have done to make his mother leave? I know you probably said no. But let me double-check that. Are you sure? Maybe she wanted a blond boy with blue eyes; maybe I teased my sister too much; maybe I didn't clean my room or wasn't smart enough. Maybe I wasn't talkative enough, tall enough or healthy enough. If you answered no, and stuck with that answer, then you are right! There is nothing that

I could have done to make my mother leave. Yet, if I told you that I have blamed myself all these years, you would understand and sympathize with me. But again, I would be wrong. There is nothing an eight-year-old boy could do that would be so terrible so as to make his mother leave. I could blame myself, but it would be entirely incorrect. Her choice to leave wasn't about me at all. It was about my mother.

Now that you know my story, let me retell the story, and as I do, I want you to start to think about the stories you tell yourself about yourself and your past. I want you to think about how you will retell those stories with you starring as the hero of that story. Once again, I want to remind you that when I talk about being a hero of your story, I am not talking about you saving anyone's life but your own; I am talking about refusing to be a victim of that story. Now, here is how I retell the story of my mother abandoning me. It goes like this: "When I was eight years old my mother sent my brother and sister and me to the store to buy some groceries. She said we could buy candy with the change and stop in the park to eat it on the way home. When we returned home, the house was empty and my mother was gone." You will notice that up to this point I have not changed the story. So far it contains the same facts and the same situation. But here's where the story and the emotional outcome of the story become significant. To continue, "There must have been something so intense going on in my mother's life that she felt the only way out was to leave. I wish her the best, and may God bless her." Same facts, same situation, different emotional outcome. In the retelling it is not about me, but about my mother. I am no longer the victim of that story, and it changes everything. The same can happen for you.

This principle applies to all stories about the past. It is not only applicable to big stories, but also to any experience that has caused you pain, sorrow, regret. Use it with any past incident that has haunted you. For instance, let's say that you went to the bank this morning. You are usually treated like their most valuable customer. They call you by name and know you and your family. But on this particular day you are treated like dirt! The teller is mean, disrespectful and demeaning.

How would you normally react? You would probably finish your business as fast as you could, and the minute you turned away from the teller, you would be on your cell phone. You'd call a friend, saying, "You are not going to believe what just happened to me! The teller at the bank just treated me like dirt!" Your next move would be to go across the street, open an account and transfer your money, letting the short negative encounter with the bank teller ruin your day. And just like that, you have become a victim! Let's not limit this to the bank. Maybe someone cut you off on the freeway, and you feared for your life. No matter the story, you can retell it so you are the hero and not the victim. Retelling the bank story could go like this: "The bank teller must have been having such a bad day that she took it out on the customers." Or you could have even asked the teller if she were having a bad day. In retelling the story in this way, you become a compassionate participant instead of an argumentative contender. By doing this, you will go from victim to hero in less than 90 seconds.

Retelling the story also works to reduce the effects of traumatic and horrific experiences as well. Not that long ago I was presenting this concept in a seminar, and I noticed a woman in the back of the room who started to tear up and then sob. Her sobbing continued through the rest of the presentation. So as soon as I was finished, I sought her out to see if I could console her. She told me that from the time she was four to eighteen years old, her father physically abused her. She had been to counseling and therapy multiple times and still felt the pain and burden of being the victim of her father's abuse. Jan was now 36 and wondering how long she would have to suffer for her father's mistakes.

Now, this brings up an important point worth pausing to explain. In retelling the story, you are not letting someone off the hook. Her father is accountable for abusing her and for his actions. Retelling the story does not absolve anyone of responsibility; it is meant as a way for you to release yourself from being a victim and free yourself from more pain.

Jan was reluctant to even try to retell the story, thinking that her father should pay for the pain and suffering he had caused. I could see the agony on her face and could feel the agony she was carrying.

I asked Jan to trust in the process and take an assignment. I asked her to take a week and try to think of any positive outcome of the experience. She looked at me like I was asking her to take poison, but once again I invited her to just give it a try. In a phone call one week later, I was taken by surprise when she said that she had indeed found one positive outcome. Jan told me that, because of the experience with her father, she is able to see when someone is about to get angry and can often diffuse the situation and be a peacemaker. She is able to do that because, in order to protect herself, she learned to sense when her father was about to beat her. Jan could see it in his face, hear it in his words and see it in his body language. Using that one positive outcome, she was then able to retell the story of her father's abuse in a way that made her no longer a complete victim. As horrible as the abuse was, Jan deserves to rise above being a victim, free to live a life with less pain. It took some time, but Jan has reported to me that learning to retell the story helped give her the benefit she had hoped for from all those years of counseling. The same can happen for you. Stop being a victim of your past and retell the story you tell yourself about what happened to you so that you are the hero of that story and no longer the victim.

Practical Tip:

To retell the story you tell yourself, you do the following:
1. Think of a story in which you are a victim.
2. Pick at least one positive outcome or put yourself in the other person's shoes.
3. Retell the story using the same facts but a different emotional outcome.
4. Repeat with a different story or a different positive outcome.
5. Continue to retell the story until you feel the pain subside.

The 90-Second Challenge

Your past, your historical markers, do not have to be a burden to you any longer. Whether your burden is heavy or light, you can rid yourself of the baggage you are carrying and become emotionally free. This emotional freedom will allow you to live more fully in the present without the past creeping in to steal your happiness, joy or satisfaction. You don't need to contaminate your present circumstances with the past. By taking the time to learn the five skills in this section, you will be able to go from being a victim of your past to a hero of your future in less than 90 seconds. Your life will change. You will feel a desire to forgive. Your self-worth will increase. You will experience daily joy and live your life with purpose. In essence, you will rediscover your true worth, your true potential and your true purpose. You will be happy!

Your Personal Assessment - Dealing with the Past

1	I often dwell on past events and feel angry because of them.
	Disagree 1 2 3 4 5 6 7 8 9 10 Agree

2	The present is never as good as the past.
	Disagree 1 2 3 4 5 6 7 8 9 10 Agree

3	I felt free and had so much fun when I was a kid. I miss being young.
	Disagree 1 2 3 4 5 6 7 8 9 10 Agree

4	High school was the best time of my life.
	Disagree 1 2 3 4 5 6 7 8 9 10 Agree

5	I feel damaged because of what has happened to me in the past.
	Disagree 1 2 3 4 5 6 7 8 9 10 Agree

6	I find it hard to let people get to know me because of the past.
	Disagree 1 2 3 4 5 6 7 8 9 10 Agree

7	I feel depressed when I can't have all the things I want.
	Disagree 1 2 3 4 5 6 7 8 9 10 Agree

8	People that have hurt me should pay for what they have done.
	Disagree 1 2 3 4 5 6 7 8 9 10 Agree

9	If life wasn't so hard I could do more. I could be better.
	Disagree 1 2 3 4 5 6 7 8 9 10 Agree

10	I wish I could have had a better childhood.
	Disagree 1 2 3 4 5 6 7 8 9 10 Agree

11	I have made a lot of mistakes that are hard to forget and get over.
	Disagree 1 2 3 4 5 6 7 8 9 10 Agree

12	I feel guilty for many of the things I have done.										
	Disagree	1	2	3	4	5	6	7	8	9	10	Agree
13	I am afraid of people learning too much about my past.										
	Disagree	1	2	3	4	5	6	7	8	9	10	Agree
14	If I had better parents and siblings I would have a better life and feel better about myself.										
	Disagree	1	2	3	4	5	6	7	8	9	10	Agree
15	If my life's story were a movie, no one would want to see it.										
	Disagree	1	2	3	4	5	6	7	8	9	10	Agree
16	I have been given a lot of chances and have blown each one.										
	Disagree	1	2	3	4	5	6	7	8	9	10	Agree
17	My childhood is so painful, I don't even like to think about it.										
	Disagree	1	2	3	4	5	6	7	8	9	10	Agree
18	So many bad things have happened to me, I find it hard to be positive about the future.										
	Disagree	1	2	3	4	5	6	7	8	9	10	Agree
19	Because of what happened to me in the past, I find it hard to trust others.										
	Disagree	1	2	3	4	5	6	7	8	9	10	Agree
20	I wish for the good old days. I was born in the wrong decade.										
	Disagree	1	2	3	4	5	6	7	8	9	10	Agree

Add up your score from the 20 questions: _____

A score of 100 or more means you have a hard time with the past and should pay serious attention to the topics presented in this section.

A score of 99 or below indicates that that you have a healthy perspective on the past.

I AM STRONG!

Part 5

Rediscover Your True Life's Purpose – Your Search for Significance

I AM STRONG!

I magine getting in your car and driving with no destination in mind. You meander from one road to another with no particular place to go. Perhaps you have actually done this to escape your present circumstances, to cool off, to clear your mind or just kill time. As a teenager I worked at a meat packing plant 45 minutes from my home. I would leave school at 11:30 in the morning to be at work by 1:00 p.m. for an 8-hour shift. I enjoyed the hard work, and having a full-time job earned me money to travel and do other things. There was a drawback: I was tired at the end of the shift, and I would often fall asleep while driving home. Do you feel as if you have worked hard all your life and made the right decisions, and you try hard to do the best you can and be the best you can be—but you feel as if you are asleep at the wheel of life? Do you feel that at one point you thought you knew where you were headed, but now you are just meandering through life without meaning or purpose? It can be a terrible feeling. For me, it took waking up in the middle of a busy intersection, having run a red light, putting not only my own life but also the lives of others in danger before I did something about it.

What will it take for you to realize that you are asleep at the wheel and do something about it? Let me use Arlene as an example. Arlene was a hard worker and did her best in all of her roles and responsibilities. She had worked for the same company for more than 20 years, was active in her church, was approaching her 26th wedding anniversary and had three successful children. Arlene was in good health for her age and exercised at least three times a week. For all intents and purposes, you would assume that Arlene was happy and content, that she was living the life she wanted live. In Arlene's own words she told me, "I feel as if I am just going through the motions. I feel like I am treading water, expending a lot of effort but not making any progress, and I feel empty inside." Ann Rand, in her book *Atlas Shrugged* writes, "What's the most depraved type of human being?...The man [or woman] without a purpose."[17] If you want to feel in control of your life, no longer driven to-and-fro by the winds of circumstance, you must have a destination! You must have a productive purpose.

You can live a meaningful life, do a lot of good works and help a lot of people but still not be living with purpose. Let me explain by sharing what I learned from Joanna. Joanna is an active and vibrant woman who volunteers at a local hospital. She loves helping others and felt that volunteering would be a good outlet for her desire to serve. What took Joanna by surprise is a phenomena referred to as compassion fatigue. Compassion fatigue can occur when, as a caregiver, you focus and invest in giving quality care without investing in self-care. Joanna, like many of you, gave tremendously, without addressing some of her own needs. As a result, the thing she likes to do most became a burden to her. While you may not be a caregiver, you may be suffering from something I call emotional deficit disorder. While not recognized by the medical community, I have witnessed emotional deficit disorder time and time again in the lives of my clients.

You could be working hard at a good job, have worthy goals and desires, experience no more nor less of the same problems we all face, and yet feel empty inside. This is a toxic emptiness because it will contaminate all of the good things you are doing and make them feel less meaningful. Consider that your life, daily activities, goals, desires and dreams are like water that flows from you – the question is what are you pouring your life into? In the book, *Life on Purpose*, Brad Swift uses this analogy to demonstrate that your true life purpose is the container into which you pour yourself. The emptiness you feel comes from missing the container completely or partially – it never fills up, leaving you with an empty feeling.[18] This becomes quite poignant with some of my more mature clients as they look back on their life, knowing that they were busy and productive, but not seeing the results they expected. If you intend to fill a bucket up with water but never put the hose in the bucket and let it run out all over the ground, you will be disappointed to discover an empty bucket.

It is time to pour your life into things that bring you meaning, purpose and significance. I have not met a single client who does not want to feel that their life has meaning and significance. What we need to do is not only discover but also create our life's purpose and then refine it. This section is meant to help you discover, create, and refine your true life's purpose, which will give you significance and meaning. Discovering your life purpose is a personal, emotional, and perhaps, even spiritual journey that isn't so much about what you do, but how and why you do it. Therefore, don't think that in order to discover your true life's purpose that you need to move to a new city, buy a new house, get a new spouse, a new job or lose weight. It is more about what is inside of you and less about your circumstances. In the movie, *It's a Wonderful Life*, George Bailey had to suffer a transformational event in order to see and ultimately feel his life's significance. Don't wait for a transformational event to compel you to find significance. You can create it, you can live it, you can reap all the benefits of a life with purpose, starting right now!

People who live a life with purpose get inspired by their work. They exude enthusiasm that emanates from the inside out. They are people of vision. These people genuinely care about their responsibilities, their colleagues, and the people they serve through their job or other activities. Their joy comes from within and is neither superficial nor forced. This is a person whose work and life are consistent with their purpose. They know why they are here and know the difference they want to make. You sense their authenticity. It's not very hard to miss them. They stand out because they live with focus, clarity of purpose and a keen sense of personal direction.

Don't assume that these people are limited to those who have lofty titles or positions. They could be almost anyone you know; a member of the cleaning crew at your office, a parent, a co-worker, sales clerk or bank teller. It doesn't matter what they are 'doing' per se. What does matter is that they operate and live their life from a central purpose. When you live with purpose it affects every aspect of your life. Job satisfaction, fulfillment, happiness, peace and love all come from the inside out, not the other way around. Purpose will help you overcome feelings of boredom and endure arduous tasks that seem meaningless on the surface. Purpose will give you energy. Knowing your central purpose will give you internal confidence, bolster your self-esteem and enable your self-worth to expand. When you discover your true life's purpose, you will begin to impact the world around you in a more positive way. Your purpose will be sensed by those whom you encounter in the same way that you feel the purposeful nature of those you encounter who live a life of purpose. Wouldn't you like to live like that?

Chapter 21

What is a Life's Purpose?

Most people define a life's purpose in terms of something you do. This 'doing' can be a job, a role, an expectation or obligation. For instance, I ask almost all of my clients, "Who are you?" The typical response has to do with what they do, not who they are. To some extent we have all been trained to identify ourselves with our jobs and our roles and think that is who we are and derive our purpose from that. Recently I asked Elaine, "Tell me who you are?" After an initial pause, with great confidence she answered, "I am a businesswoman, wife, and mother of three beautiful children." Elaine's response is not wrong, per se, but it told me that she identifies with the roles she has taken on.

I think we can all agree that our roles are important. But there is a danger with deriving our purpose from and identifying ourselves in terms of the roles we play in life. If you identify with the role of a businesswoman and then lose your job or your business, you may feel lost and without purpose. We all need to remember that a job is important, and it is important to do your best at whatever you do. But a job is a means to an end, not the end itself. The same is true as Elaine's children grow up and leave home. She may feel increasingly lost and empty as her role as a mother transforms and changes over time. These things happen to all of us and are more devastating if we derive our purpose from what we do or from a role. What we do will change, our roles change, our aspirations and goals change as well. Your true life's purpose should be more inherent and internal.

We most often do things to have something. We work hard to own a home, to have financial security and to acquire more possessions. The irony is that our possessions possess us. The more we have, the more we want; and the more we want, the more we have to do to get what we want. This creates a vicious cycle of doing and having. This cycle can become so powerful that we buy into the lie that our purpose is *to do* – so that we can *have*. We start to believe that our purpose is to be the 'breadwinner,' the 'provider,' the 'problem solver,' or the 'giver.' Don't confuse your 'doing' with your purpose. Surely, your true life's purpose will include some amount of doing, but it is not the doing that is your purpose. Your true life's purpose is much greater than what you do. When we allow our purpose to be defined by what we do, it is a purpose created by default.

Don't get me wrong. You have purpose right now. It may not be the purpose you would create for yourself; it is likely one that you have inherited. I recently met with Melissa who described herself as a compassionate giver. When I asked her what or how she gave, she explained that she made sure to be there for her children, to give them anything they needed. At first I assumed that she was referring to small children who could not fend for themselves, but I was surprised to learn that her children were ages 28 and 31. She had become the emotional counselor, the bank, roadside assistance, and day care provider to her daughters. Melissa is a giver and had been a giver so long that she had trained those around her to count on her to give and give and give. While giving is good, allowing yourself to be taken advantage of or, worse, defining your life purpose around this, is not healthy.

Melissa's overwhelming feeling of emptiness got the best of her and threw her into depression that had lasted for more than 12 months. She came to me as a last ditch effort to overcome her depression and emotional numbness. As we discussed her situation, it became clear that she felt obligated to continue the role, which she defined as her purpose, because that is what her daughters and others expected of her. The expectation to give was so strong that Melissa accepted it as her purpose in life. The problem with this kind of purpose is that it is

I AM STRONG!

unsustainable. When you give and give and give without context of a larger purpose and without self-care, you end up giving what you don't have and end up emotionally overdrawn. You start to live from one crisis to the next. I call this the 'crash and burn' cycle. Melissa had allowed her purpose to be defined by her past, by her role of mother, and by the expectations of others. Living according to an inherited purpose, or a purpose acquired by default, creates internal conflict that will inevitably surface and cause distress. This conflict may rest dormant for many years, only to become severe later in life or when you finally have had enough. In many cases this can be the source of a mid-life crisis, as you wake up one day to realize the road you have been traveling will not get you where you want to go. While a mid-life crisis has become a cliché, it is nonetheless serious and can be severe. The severity can largely be based on your sense of purpose.

You have a purpose! You are significant! You may not realize your true life's purpose yet, and you may not be able to visualize it right this moment. But it is there just waiting to burst out and be fulfilled. Think of a fat and happy caterpillar hanging upside down on the plant eating leaf after leaf. Can he visualize himself as more than a caterpillar whose purpose and destiny is to become a stunning butterfly that pollinates flowers, which will beautify the countryside? Though he may not be able to see it, it is nevertheless his destiny. What will be your purpose? What is the significance you are searching for? It is inside of you, just waiting for you to crack open the cocoon you are living in and spread your wings.

"What do you want to be when you grow up?" Every one of us at one time or another has contemplated this question. I remember my own father asking me what I wanted to be when I grew up. I have asked my children the same thing. I have heard many of my clients ask themselves this same question, realizing that they have expended much time and effort living life without knowing what they really want to be when they grow up. The question itself has become part of our American lore and has a nostalgic ring to it.

It's an innocent question that can provide some motivation and help a child set goals. Not long ago I attended an award ceremony for a friend receiving a prestigious award as a city attorney. As part of her speech she told of watching a presidential inauguration when she was eight years old. She asked her father what the men on TV did for a living. Her father replied that most of them were lawyers. She said that she wanted to become an attorney when she grew up, and she did. Just this past week I received an email from a reader who told me that as a young girl she watched soap operas with her mother after school. In one of the shows there was a woman who worked in an architectural firm who was always carrying around blueprints and drawings. For some reason she felt a connection with this woman. She ended up working for almost 30 years in an engineering firm where her primary responsibility was to manage blueprints and other engineering drawings.

While the question, "What do you want to be when you grow up" is innocent enough, it causes us to focus on the 'what' as our life purpose. Focusing on a career or a profession is important, but we need to remember it is a means to an end, not the end itself. I have met far too many career professionals who literally lose their identity and purpose to their work. So for our intent here discussing how to arrive at our true life's purpose, a more appropriate question is, "Who do you want to be when you grow up?" Now the focus is on the who, not the what. We can determine who we are and follow that purpose regardless of what we do. So who do you want to be when you grow up? Now is the time to decide!

Chapter 22

The Benefits of Living your Life's Purpose

There is a growing body of research on the subject of having something to live for or having a reason to get out of bed in the morning. *AARP Magazine*, a magazine dedicated to serving the needs of people 50 and older wrote, "A 2005 study that followed 12,640 middle-aged Hungarians found that those who felt their lives had meaning had significantly lower rates of cancer and heart disease than did those who didn't feel this way."[19] In the same article, Dan Beuttner, author of *The Blue Zones*, said that "having a reason to get out of bed was a common trait in many of the worlds' centenarians." Harold G. Koenig, M.D., professor of psychiatry and behavioral sciences at Duke University Medical Center, was quoted in the article as stating, "People who feel their life is part of a larger plan and are guided by their spiritual values have stronger immune systems, lower blood pressure, a lower risk of heart attack and cancer, and heal faster and live longer." Having a purpose will keep you healthier and make you live longer. Many studies indicate that people who retire early have a higher mortality rate. If you have a worthy purpose to provide you direction and significance, then it is best to continue working as long as you are able. This does not mean you have to work forever in order to live longer. It speaks to the importance of having an abiding sense of purpose and significance. Following are some of the amazing benefits you can experience by discovering and living your true life's purpose:

Focus and direction: Living without a purpose leaves you feeling as if you have little or no control over your own life. When you don't have a destination in mind, you are likely to be tossed to-and-fro by any whim or become distracted by seemingly good things. Discovering and living your life's purpose gives focus and definition to your life. You won't be as easily derailed. It will increase your determination, confidence and commitment, which will strengthen your power to actualize your goals.

Easier decision making: Once I discovered and articulated my true life's purpose, it was easier to see where I had been and where I wanted to go. This made it easier to make decisions. The road of life has many side streets that look inviting and opportunistic. Having true purpose allows you to stay focused and discern the opportunities that best support your purpose from those that don't. For example, I have a good friend, Sheila, who is quite outgoing and charismatic and could probably sell ice to winter travelers in Alaska. She is constantly approached by well meaning friends and family to join their latest network marketing opportunity. Because Sheila knows her purpose, she is able to simply say, "No thank you. That is not the path I am on." When you know your 'path,' you don't need to waste time investigating every opportunity that comes you way. You make better, more informed decisions with wiser judgment.

Confidence: When you have a purpose and know it is your true life's purpose, confidence will emanate from the inside out. Everyone you encounter will feel and recognize it in you. If you have spent any time people-watching in a big city, you can quickly point out who is lost, who is depressed, who knows where they are going, and who feels good about themselves. When you have a purpose, you stand taller, walk deliberately, and your voice changes as well. People respect you more and will give you more opportunity to speak because it is clear that you know what you want and where you are going.

Passion: I am not referring to passion in a physical or sexual sense.

Discovering and living your life's purpose adds passion—spirit, drive and zeal—to your life. This will lift your mood and make you feel more energetic. It will elevate your contribution to the community, your work and your family.

Fulfillment: Living a life without purpose is like treading water, hoping you make it to the other side. Albert Einstein is quoted as saying, "Insanity is doing the same thing over and over again and expecting a different result." Having purpose, and especially a true life's purpose, as opposed to one you have inherited by default, makes you sane. You are no longer treading water in the sea of life; you are now on a boat moving forward with a wake of fulfillment following. You will feel meaning enter your life the instant you discover your purpose.

Integrity: Doing the right things for the right reasons is one definition of integrity. Living with purpose that is consistent with your values and morals will increase your integrity. You will intuitively know the right things to do and be able to do them for the right reasons. This is the essence of value-based living. This will strengthen your moral compass, which gives you courage to stand up for truth and right.

Flow: One of the most profound benefits of knowing and living your life purpose is the increased opportunity to experience flow. Flow can be described as a mental state in which a person is fully engaged in an activity or task, often completely involved to the point of losing awareness of time passing. This single-minded immersion in the present is marked by an energized focus and heightened ability to learn and perform. Depression, anxiety, nervousness and a lack of purpose are all obstacles to experiencing flow. The concept of flow can also be extended beyond an activity or task to entire phases of a person's life. Feelings of fulfillment and enjoyment accompany a person who is in the flow.

I AM STRONG!

Chapter 23

How to Discover, Develop and Live with Purpose

I would like to introduce you to a simple formula that will help you discover, implement and live your true life's purpose. The formula is found in this simple sentence: _**A** **T**rue **P**urpose **I**ncludes **S**trengths, **G**ifts, **V**alues and **B**eliefs_. The first letter of each word in this sentence is an element of the formula that will help you in your journey to discover a life with purpose and to eventually be able to write your true life's purpose.

> **A is for Accomplish** – What would you like to accomplish?
> **T is for Talents** – What are your talents?
> **P is for Passion** – What are you passionate about?
> **I is for Intent** – What is your real intent?
> **S is for Strengths** – What are your key strengths?
> **G is for Gifts** – What are your gifts?
> **V is for Values** – What are your values?
> **B is for Beliefs** – What are your core beliefs?

Your true life's purpose is a reflection of who you really are, a reflection of your divine nature, your core values, your spirituality and your deepest desire to make a contribution to this world and have a positive impact on the people around you. As you can see, each letter in the formula represents a subject and a question. As you answer those questions with your heart (and not so much with your mind), you arrive at a good idea of what your purpose is so you can write it down and start to live it. You can use the worksheet at the end of this section or take out a piece of paper and jot down notes and answers to the questions as you read on.

A is for Accomplish: What would you like to accomplish in your life-time? I would like you to spend a few minutes pondering and reflecting on what it is you feel you are meant to accomplish here on this earth in this time period. If resources, time and money were endless and all obstacles and limitations were removed, how would you occupy your time? Another similar exercise is to write your own obituary noting the things you have accomplished. Would your obituary be a list of jobs you had? Contributions to society and the world at large? Reflect and write it down.

Applying A is for Accomplish:

After pondering what you would like to accomplish with your life, fill in the blanks:

❭ If money were of no concern, and if I had what I truly needed, I would spend my time _____

_____

_____because I _____

_____.

T is for Talents: What are your talents? For this question you are not to worry about sounding conceited or arrogant. I am asking you to do a truthful and objective reflection on the many talents you have. Don't get caught up in the typical talents only, such as music, singing or gardening. I want you to seriously consider the intangible talents that are evident or dormant, just waiting for the chance to emerge and become a source of fulfillment and satisfaction. With most of my clients we spend a good deal of time on this element, as I have found that most people are simply unaware of the many talents they have. My eldest son is a gifted musician and felt that was his talent. When he was 18 he created and produced his first CD. He discovered a talent for project management that has since become a great source of satisfaction to him. What are your hidden and perhaps not-so-obvious talents?

Applying T is for Talents:

Take a few minutes right now and write down what you think your top talents are by answering this question:

》 Think of a powerful and peak experience in your life where you felt everything turned out just right. What did you contribute to that experience?

1. _____
2. _____
3. _____
4. _____

P is for Passion: What are you are passionate about? I would like you to think about the things you have done in the past that made you feel whole, complete and fulfilled. Try not to think of awards or recognition, as this is not about external validation. Think of events when you were in the flow or immersed in something that filled you up or that you thoroughly enjoyed. Ponder the times in your life when you felt inherently worthy of happiness and satisfaction. Your passion may be playing the piano, doing crafts, exercising or reading. You may be passionate about supporting cancer research, helping new mothers care for their babies or supporting literacy in your community. Those are all things to consider when writing down your passions and the feelings you have when you are actively engaged in those passions.

Applying P is for Passion:

It is important to know what you care most about. Try not to think in term of things or roles you play. What is deep inside of you waiting to be released?

❭ What are you most passionate about?

1. _____
2. _____
3. _____
4. _____

I is for Intent: When considering your life purpose, it is important to assess your intent, which comes from within. Whether you notice or not, your intentions drive your life and are much stronger than a want or a desire. For example, consider these two sentences: "I want to go on a bike ride," and "I intend to go on bike ride." The intent statement carries more energy than simply saying you want to do something. The same is true in terms of your true life purpose. To want to be honest, caring and charitable is admirable and worthy of your attention. But to restate that desire in the form of an intent, "I intend to be more charitable," will help align your beliefs and actions in a way that will strengthen your ability to become what you intend. What is it you intend for your life? Can you describe your life's intent in one sentence? While you may find it difficult to determine your intent, it may be easier to start by considering why you are here on this earth and what your legacy will be. Articulating this intent will have the added benefit of enabling you to live your life with real intent. That includes being present and living in real time. You will feel your real intent as you increase your self-worth and start to feel inherently worthy of love, happiness, fulfillment and satisfaction. Real intent grows as you forgive others and unburden yourself from the past that is holding you back.

Applying I is for Intent:

Think of your intent for your life. Think of this as your higher reason behind what you hope to accomplish in your life (according to what you wrote down in the first step).

❯ What is my real intent? _____

_____

_____

_____

S is for Strengths: Your true life's purpose should come from a position of strength, not weakness. I know that it may be in vogue to identify and work on your weaknesses in an effort to make personal growth, but for now consider the great strengths you have and how you can use them to make a contribution to your happiness and to the happiness of the people around you. I have found that most people are unable to articulate their strengths, and to help you, I highly recommend the book *Now, Discover Your Strengths* by Marcus Buckingham and Donald O. Clifton. Each copy of their book includes a code that allows you to go on-line and take a Strengths Assessment. The answers you give in the assessment are then compared to the answers of millions of others in order to identify your key signature strengths. I have taken the assessment multiple times over the past several years, and my key strengths have not changed. I know what my strengths are and you can too. These are the strengths you should focus on when considering your true life's purpose.

Another way to assess your strengths is to ask several people who know you to share what they consider your top five strengths. You may be surprised at how many great and wonderful strengths others recognize in you.

Practical Tip:

To apply S is for Strengths, ask at least three people who know you well to tell you what your greatest strengths are. Have them list at least five:

1. _____
2. _____
3. _____
4. _____
5. _____

G is for Gifts: What are your gifts? We all have gifts. There is not one person on this planet who does not have many more gifts than he or she is aware of. Have you been blessed with great intuition and insight? Perhaps you have the gift of unconditional compassion or the gift of service to others. You might have the gift of self-discipline, speaking, wisdom or friendship. These are all gifts that most people don't consider. Your gifts are more about who you are than what you do. When we use our gifts to make a contribution to those we love and to society in general, we feel peace and flow. Your purpose should take your great gifts into consideration.

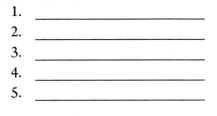

Applying G is for Gifts:

Gifts are different from strengths. Think of character traits that are unique to you. Are you nurturing? Compassionate? Do you have an ability to see both the details and big picture at the same time? Are you creative? Do you have a healthy, natural good sense of humor?

Write down at least five gifts. Don't worry if this is hard to do. It usually takes some time to consider what your gifts are.

1. _____
2. _____
3. _____
4. _____
5. _____

V is for Values: Consider both what you value most in life and what your morals are. Your true life purpose must be consistent with your values and your morals. Otherwise, you will create internal conflict that will sabotage your life purpose and diminish the value, satisfaction, fulfillment and peace you can experience. What are your values? What do you stand for? Take the time to think about this and then write down a short list of what you value most. In an effort to discover your true life purpose, you will need to get to know yourself from the inside out. Because a true life purpose should focus on who you are, not so much on what you do, it is important to understand your values. If you value honesty and integrity, then your purpose must align with those values. These are not only values in the sense of character attributes but also those intangible things that are most precious to you, such as kindness or sincerity.

Applying V is for Values:

We all have values that we live by, but seldom do we take the time to ponder them and write them down. Take the time now to identify your values and put them down on paper:

1. _____
2. _____
3. _____
4. _____
5. _____

B is for Beliefs: What are your core beliefs? This may be a tough question for some of you who don't yet believe in yourself, your strengths, your gifts or your talents. You might want to spend more time in the previous sections so that you can believe in your ability to do great things and to be a great person. However, this is more about your beliefs as they relate to your life and what you want to accomplish. For example, do you believe that you are here for a purpose, perhaps a divine and God-given purpose, to accomplish great things? Do you believe that your actions make a difference? Those are the beliefs I am referring to, but you should also include your religious and spiritual beliefs as well.

Applying B is for Beliefs:

Beliefs are critical to your life purpose because if you don't believe you can accomplish what you wrote in the first step, discovering your true life purpose will be that much harder. Do you believe in yourself? What else do you believe?

1. _____
2. _____
3. _____
4. _____
5. _____

Other important factors to consider

Besides the formula above that will help you contemplate the key aspects of your life purpose, there are other factors to consider. One very important factor is your uniqueness. While I don't necessarily mean that you stand out in a crowd, I am referring to what your life has taught you. Here are some other questions that will add color, definition and depth to your journey to discover your life purpose.

What were the circumstances when you felt the most challenged in your life? This can be a specific event or a period of intense adversity. The question is not necessarily about what happened, but about how you got through it and what you discovered about yourself. When I was diagnosed with cancer the second time, I didn't feel worthy of the trial and knew in my heart there was something significant I needed to learn through the experience. That learning did not happen until several years later when I realized the depth of my struggle and the internal strength I never knew I had. Think about your trials, challenges, and adversity in terms of what you have learned and how you are now better because of it. Doing this will provide great clues about who you are.

When did you feel most alive, most excited and most in the moment? Can you describe the circumstances and remember what you were doing, what you were thinking and how you felt? When did you feel consumed with motivation and desire and at the same time felt tremendous peace? These are likely instances when you were in the flow, and if you can analyze the situation in such a way as to create more self-awareness of the positive moments in your life, you'll be able to repeat the process so you can be in the flow more often.

What do you care most about? This is not just an exercise in setting priorities but a sincere question about what you care about most. This is closely related to what you feel passionate about. The reason this is a separate question is to help you reduce conflicts between your passions and your priorities. For example, if you are passionate about the spread of AIDS in Africa but care most about time with your family, they may be in conflict and, thus, will create a conflict of interest with your life purpose. At the same time, discovering, defining and living your life purpose does not mean you need to quit your job, move to a new city or seek a new partner. Your purpose can combine what you feel passionate about and what care most about.

What are the hopes, prayers and vision you hold for the world? When considering your life purpose, another important factor is how you relate to the world in which you live. Your purpose, the difference you can make and are already making in this world should coincide with your hopes, dreams, prayers and vision you hold for the world at large.

Who are you and what can others count on you for? This question also relates to the discussion about your strengths. It is important to consider the ways in which others rely upon you. What do they count on you to do and to be? This is not meant to be a discussion about dependence, obligation or manipulation. It is meant to cause you to take a moment and think about what others see in you and the difference you are already making in this world.

Chapter 24

Comfort Zones and Opposition

Though you may not think so, you are already living a life with purpose. Chances are it is not a purpose that you have chosen but one you have grown into by default. This purpose you are living may be merely to get by or to fly under the radar. Yet deep inside you are longing for significance, meaning and purpose. You can have all of that, but it will not come without opposition. For the past several years I am fortunate to be living my dream, but I never realized how hard it is to live your dream. While it is not drudgery and is extremely satisfying, it still requires hard work. Think of it like taking a hike in the most beautiful place in the world. There may be beauty all around you, but you still need to put one foot in front of the other and climb. In many cases your true life purpose will choose you; chances are you have already rejected it more than once. Now is the time to pay attention to the obstacles and opposition of living a life according to your true life purpose.

One of the biggest obstacles will be your own comfort zone. Judy is a perfect example. Judy had been quite content with her life. She was content in her marriage and with their five children and was looking forward to being an empty-nester. As much as the idea of being an empty-nester appealed to Judy, when that phase of her life arrived she felt that she was not living up to her potential and knew that she needed to contribute something more. This feeling was so powerful that she came to me for help and guidance in figuring out what the 'more' could be. She had a hard time articulating it, other than describing a nagging or a nudge to help the less fortunate. Judy had been raised in meager circumstances and felt so grateful for the life of abundance she now enjoyed that she wanted to help those who were struggling.

After Judy and I went through the previous exercises and the questions, she felt directed to become a foster parent to disabled children. It both scared her and energized her at the same time. It took a lot to convince her husband that she felt this was her true life purpose. Finally, her husband agreed, and Judy began living the purpose that was revealed to her. Is she busy? Yes! Is it hard? Yes! But she feels truly blessed, and it has had a positive impact on the whole family. Judy needed to step out of her comfort zone into a life of purpose. Your true life purpose may not require something as drastic. Be aware that it will be met with opposition from your own self-indictment and likely from others as well. Stay true, stay strong, and have the courage to accept your true life purpose and start to live a fulfilling life.

You may also experience opposition in the form of having a busy mind. In order to devote the effort needed to discover your true life purpose, you will need focus and attention. For most of you this will be a challenge in and of itself, merely based on how busy your mind is. One assignment I give most of my clients is to find a few minutes each day to be still both in body and in mind. This is the precursor to meditation. I have found that as my clients are able to find the time each day, even if for just a few minutes, to be quiet, to calm their body and still their minds, they are more likely to adopt a practice of meditation and receive clarity, solutions and wisdom from within themselves. Your true life purpose will be revealed to you as you go through the previous exercises and questions, particularly as you ponder the significance of the answers in a calm and peaceful setting. It is likely that your purpose has been shouting to you, but you haven't been able to hear it.

Linda could barely sleep because of the chatter in her mind. Every night when she lay down, her mind began to race, thinking of all the things she didn't get done and all the things she needed to do the next day. To say she was burning the candle at both ends would be an understatement. There were simply not enough hours in the day or enough mental capacity to handle it all. When I asked Linda to set aside 15 minutes a day for quiet reflection, she looked at me like I was crazy. She appeared to be thinking, "Did you not hear what I just said? I am too busy to do anything else. I don't even have time to go the bathroom!" Nevertheless, I persevered, and week after week strongly suggested she take the time. I wanted to help her to see that it would be the best 15 minutes of her day, and that she would get more done in less time, that things would miraculously start to fall off her plate instead of falling onto her plate. I am not sure if it was my relentless suggestion or if it was out of desperation, but Linda finally agreed to the 15 minutes a day. Linda was an overachiever, and I knew that once she committed, it would not be just 15 minutes but at least 20 and more like 30!

Within one week you would not have recognized Linda. She had become transformed and a believer in miracles. It was as if her life took a slow-down pill. She felt less frantic and hurried, less busy, and more at peace. Sure, she had a ways to go, but the seven-day transformation was amazing. The most awesome part is that she was finally able to see that she had been so busy *doing* that she could not *be*. This was the first step to having her true life purpose revealed to her. Today Linda uses her great skills and talents in the nonprofit sector. She loves it. She is still busy, but the context of her 'busy-ness' is more meaningful and significant. Don't let the busy-ness of life be so loud that you can't hear the beckoning of your true life purpose.

The hardest thing to contend with is the obstacle of your own negative self-talk. Anytime you start to contemplate you true life purpose, you will excite the antibodies that have been planted into your dialogue by your programming and experiences. Just like Judy, there were many reasons she could come up with for not opening her heart and her home to disabled orphans. If she listened to those voices exclusively, she would not be living her purpose like she is today. Your own negative voice will be the loudest opposition you will hear. It is time to think in terms of what you were born to do, not what you are doing because it is convenient and what you are used to.

Stop listening to the litany of derogatory comments you make about yourself every day. Learn to talk tenderly to yourself. I know this may appear silly and awkward, but I want you to talk to yourself in the same tone and care you would use to talk to an infant or a small child. You don't have to practice this long before you change the tone of inner-voice, but don't change the positive, nurturing nature of your self-talk. Tell yourself that you are worthy of a true life purpose, of direction and meaning. Tell yourself you are capable, wonderful and able to do what you were born to do.

If there is one category of person who will likely have the hardest time discovering their true life purpose, it is the 'know-it-all.' You know this person, and perhaps know them quite well. This is the person who is so full of their own ideas and opinions that there is no room for even the inkling of inspiration to lead them to discover their true life purpose. Are you that person? Is your mind and soul so full of yourself that you can't see beyond what you think you already know? To some degree, discovering your true life purpose requires tolerance for uncertainty, faith, and the ability to believe in the intangible. It may require you to take risks, to become vulnerable and to admit you don't know everything. Your true life purpose may challenge what already know and cause you to learn something new and to learn more about yourself. Take that leap of faith, set aside trusting in only what you see, and learn to be led by a greater power, a power that is beyond you. For me, this greater power is God. For you it may be the power of the universe or another higher power. Nevertheless, take that step into the unknown and believe you are here to make a difference, a real and powerful, positive difference.

Perhaps you think you need to get your life in order first before you embark on anything close to resembling your true life purpose. I am not suggesting that you should be irresponsible and abandon your responsibilities in pursuit of your true life purpose. I am suggesting, however, that you don't need to be 'all together' in order to pursue it. Somewhere along that continuum is the right answer. There are definitely some real decisions that need to be made. Let's say you are currently studying accounting but feel the need to enter the health-care field as a nurse. You may want to finish your current semester before changing direction, so as to preserve your grade point average; but don't let that get in your way. Your true life purpose, by nature, is a longer term pursuit and should be given the reverence and respect it deserves. You don't have to be perfect, get all your ducks in a row first, or wait until the perfect time to discover what you were meant to do. You can start now. Right now!

The last obstacle to discovering and living your true life purpose is probably the most significant and the hardest to deal with. Along with others, I call this, 'settling.' After trying hard time and time again to break out of a rut or reach for the stars, only to fall on your face, there is a strong temptation to just settle in and accept that "maybe this is all there is," or "maybe this is just as good as it gets." We still wish for more but become complacent and apathetic about our chances of ever amounting to anything. I can't tell you how many times I have heard the words, "Why should I even try?" Are those words you say? Are you suffering from complacency because you have failed in the past, thinking that you are doomed for a life of failure? You are giving into the gravitational pull of mediocrity, thinking that it is easier to give in than to try. On some level I can completely understand and sympathize. But the truth is – settling is not easier. Remember that living your true life's purpose will endow you with strength, energy, and even improved health, which alone will make things easier. Don't settle for less! Keep trying! Don't settle for the misery, loneliness, lack of fulfillment and sadness that you feel. You can change all of that by discovering, creating and living a life of purpose.

I AM STRONG!

Chapter 25:

Bringing It All Together

Now that you have the foundation of understanding what a true life purpose is, and now that you have assessed your values, ideals, wants and desires, it is time to take the next step: putting it all together into an actionable and workable true life purpose. So many people get this far, only to stop with fear of choosing the wrong purpose. My answer to that is that if you select the wrong purpose, you will know quickly and be able to make refinements. A life purpose is not a static statement that is meant to be engraved on a charm and worn on a bracelet. It is a statement of direction and meaning that can be refined over time to evolve as your true life purpose. Going back to the beginning of this section and using the analogy of driving, at first your life purpose may be like saying, "I want to drive to Chicago." And after driving for a bit in that direction, you can become clearer in determining the exact address where you want to end up. Start more general and become more specific over time as you grow, learn and discover more about yourself.

A true life purpose should be far from a goal of obtaining material possessions. Certainly in some circles, the mantra of "the one with the most toys wins" is fun and humorous, but it should not be your true life purpose. While the acquisition of new possessions may be the result of your true life purpose, it should not be the purpose itself. Investing the core of your heart, time and energy in the accumulation or maintenance of material possessions represents a shallow and unproductive purpose that, in my experience, creates more misery in the long run. At the same time, don't think that your true life purpose needs to be so altruistic as to require you to live a life of poverty and abstention of pleasure. That is certainly not the case. While I strongly recommend that you stray from expressing your true life purpose in terms of a monetary figure, you can certainly pursue the purpose of being able to help others financially or in other philanthropic activities. Those are all good. Do not shy away from riches because you think that money is evil. Money is a valuable resource in pursuing your true life purpose. Just keep it in perspective and remember that material goods and money are a means to an end, not the end itself.

You may want to start thinking about and choosing a daily purpose that can change and adapt each day as you discover more about yourself and what brings you the ultimate satisfaction. You don't need to wait until you have completed all the assessments and questions in this section to begin. Start small and learn. One way to do this is to create a daily Affirm-Action. This is something that I use with the majority of my clients to help them ease into the process of choosing and then writing a true life purpose. An Affirm-Action is a simple action-oriented affirmation that you set for the day. An Affirm-Action always begins with the words "Today I will…." followed by a statement of purpose. Here are a few examples:

Today I will be more forgiving.

Today I will reach out to an old friend and tell them how much I appreciate them.

Today I will eat more vegetables.

Today I will smile at everyone I encounter.

Today I will talk tenderly to myself.

Today I will give people a break.

Today I will accept my partner for who he/she is without judgment.

Making Affirm-Actions Work for You

Write an action-oriented affirmation on a sticky note or on your mirror with lipstick so that you can recall it throughout the day. You will be surprised at the positive emotions you will feel by having a purpose for the day. Try it for 7, 14, or 30 days.

My recommendation is to follow this simple four-step process to discover and live your true life purpose:

1. Write it.
2. Live it.
3. Evaluate it.
4. Refine it.

Imagine the power and clarity that will come by writing and doing daily Affirm-Actions that support your life purpose. Remember, your true life purpose will be revealed to you as you go through the process.

Write your True Life Purpose

To help you discover your true life purpose, I suggest you start with the self-assessment and inventory at the end of this section. This will help measure where you are in the process and determine whether you simply need to refine or clarify your true life's purpose or do more triage to discover, develop and live that purpose. A life purpose is not something you pull out of a hat, nor is it something you can achieve by filling out forms or templates on the internet. It is a personal journey that requires some self-awareness and self-reflection. It is intentional that this section comes after the previous sections on self-worth, forgiving and overcoming your past. Your life purpose will be more significant and solid when you approach the discovery from a position of emotional freedom and high self-worth. If you jumped to this section of the book first, I highly recommend that you now go back and spend some time in the previous three sections before continuing.

The goal of this section is to provide you with the tools and determination to no longer live an ad hoc life, but to live on purpose and to live your life's true purpose. Let me now provide some guidance to help you actually write this down and start the process. With the answers from the previous exercises, fill in the blanks below.

My purpose is to be _____,

_____, _____,

by living a life of _____

so that I can _____

_____

_____.

To help you further, let me provide some real examples from a few of my clients who have taken this process seriously enough to reap the benefits.

My purpose is to be an <u>honest, loving and kind woman</u> by living a life of <u>love and service to others</u> so that I can <u>help others see their true nature and divinity</u>.

My purpose is to be <u>sincere, loving and true</u> by living a <u>healthy, active</u> life of <u>giving to others</u> so that I can <u>be a greater servant of God</u>.

My purpose is to be of <u>service to those who have experienced the loss of a loved one</u> so that I can <u>help them feel loved and wanted</u>.

My purpose is to be <u>forgiving, hard working, and vulnerable</u> by living a life of <u>caring for and nurturing disabled children</u> so that I can <u>lift and inspire their hearts and souls</u>.

My purpose is to be <u>the best I can and to participate in self-care</u> by living a life of <u>integrity, service and support</u> so I can <u>be there for those who are in need</u>.

These are just examples using the template that I have provided you. Don't think that you need to follow the words of the template exactly, but use them as a guide to discover, develop, live and refine your true life purpose. You can be as specific or as general as you want. Remember, this is a journey, a process, a refinement of what you are meant to do.

Your True Life Purpose Self-Evaluation

1	I seldom feel like I am wandering through life without direction.
	Disagree 1 2 3 4 5 6 7 8 9 10 Agree

2	I no longer have a deep sense that there is something in store for me that I'm unable to find.
	Disagree 1 2 3 4 5 6 7 8 9 10 Agree

3	I am able to list my five greatest strengths and talents.
	Disagree 1 2 3 4 5 6 7 8 9 10 Agree

4	I can articulate what the most important aspect of my life is.
	Disagree 1 2 3 4 5 6 7 8 9 10 Agree

5	I am clear about what my life purpose is.
	Disagree 1 2 3 4 5 6 7 8 9 10 Agree

6	I demonstrate my life purpose in how I make decisions.
	Disagree 1 2 3 4 5 6 7 8 9 10 Agree

7	I recognize the contribution I make to others as I live my life with purpose.
	Disagree 1 2 3 4 5 6 7 8 9 10 Agree

8	I live a value-based life rather than a materialistic life.
	Disagree 1 2 3 4 5 6 7 8 9 10 Agree

9	My life is shaped by my life purpose, rather than by what others expect of me or think I should be.
	Disagree 1 2 3 4 5 6 7 8 9 10 Agree

10	I see the simple abundance around me and acknowledge it each day.
	Disagree 1 2 3 4 5 6 7 8 9 10 Agree

11	My life is free of unnecessary clutter and complexities, and I seldom feel overwhelmed.
	Disagree 1 2 3 4 5 6 7 8 9 10 Agree

12	I regularly express my gratitude for the bounty of life that is all around me.
	Disagree 1 2 3 4 5 6 7 8 9 10 Agree

13	I regularly reflect that the best things in life are free.
	Disagree 1 2 3 4 5 6 7 8 9 10 Agree

14	I regularly take time for self-care and self-reflection.
	Disagree 1 2 3 4 5 6 7 8 9 10 Agree

15	I have plenty of time to devote to my family, friends, and community.
	Disagree 1 2 3 4 5 6 7 8 9 10 Agree

16	I have a rich and satisfying spiritual life.
	Disagree 1 2 3 4 5 6 7 8 9 10 Agree

17	I have taken time to explore my beliefs in order to be certain they are my own choice, rather than defaulting to what others think I should believe.
	Disagree 1 2 3 4 5 6 7 8 9 10 Agree

18	I have established my home as a peaceful place where I can rejuvenate physically, emotionally, and spiritually.
	Disagree 1 2 3 4 5 6 7 8 9 10 Agree

19	I feel a deep sense of security, and I am seldom fearful of not having 'enough' of anything.
	Disagree 1 2 3 4 5 6 7 8 9 10 Agree

20	I realize that my work and my roles (Mother, Father, Sibling, etc…) do not define my life purpose.
	Disagree 1 2 3 4 5 6 7 8 9 10 Agree

Now add up your score and write it down here:_____

Based on your score, you can determine what category best describes where you are right now:

20 – 60: Wandering
60 – 90: Hanging on
90 - 120: Striving

120 – 160: Competent
160 – 200: Living with purpose

Part 6:

Experience Joy Every Day

I AM STRONG!

Having completed the first four sections, you are now ready and able to experience the greatest benefit of I AM STRONG – experiencing joy every day. Joy is an interesting topic that is often reserved for the feelings one has through a spiritual experience or for only the most positive experiences. I believe you can experience some amount of joy every day. Joy is a form of happiness resulting from meaningful positive emotions. Not that long ago I was visiting Heidelberg, Germany and stopped in a Starbucks to take a break from the cold. It was December, and the Heidelberg Christmas Market was in full swing. Booths had been set up in several town squares, and people were milling about socializing with friends and enjoying the local fare of langos, bratwurst and sweets. I took a seat near the window so that I could people-watch in comfort. However, it was not the scene outside that caught my attention but a woman across the room taking great pleasure in her hot drink. She clasped the hot mug with both hands, held it up to take in the aroma, and then would take a small sip and sigh as she put the cup down on the table. Either she had never had a drink taste so good or it had been a long time since she had such a drink. Regardless, the look on her face, her body language and the sighing clearly communicated that she was enjoying it. I really mean she was in-joy with it.

When was the last time you were in-joy or joy was in you? If you had asked me that question a few years ago, I would have answered by telling you my only daughter's wedding in December 1999. Even as I write this section, mere thoughts of that day bring me joy. I remember leaving the temple where she was married, feeling like the world around me was more beautiful. My heart was full of awe and wonder. Although it was the middle of winter, it felt as if it were spring. Instead of bitter cold I felt warmth. I had greater love for everything and everyone around me. It was a tremendous feeling. However, just one hour later, as we hurried to the restaurant for the luncheon and then to the church to attend to other wedding chores, I noticed that the intense feelings of joy had left me, and I longed for its return. But now that feeling of joy, the joy that I feel just remembering my daughter's wedding, is no longer an isolated or rare event for me. I now feel that same joy on a regular and daily basis and so can you. Joy does not have to be isolated to rare events or when everything turns out just right. You can be in-joy in this very minute, regardless of your circumstances or your situation.

Let me share another experience with you to demonstrate what I mean. A few weeks ago I broke a tooth. I was not in pain, except that the ragged edge of the broken tooth tore up the side of my tongue and was quite uncomfortable. I was traveling at the time and had no way to see the dentist for at least a week. When I arrived at the dentist's office, the receptionist asked how I was doing. Without hesitation I said I was having a great day. That puzzled her. She then asked how I could be having a great day with a broken tooth and a tongue torn up on one side. My answer was simple. I said, "I just have a broken tooth, not a rotten day." Do you let small things get in your way of being in-joy? Are you waiting for great things to happen before you can feel intense happiness and peace? You don't need to.

While joy can be described as the happiest of emotions, I am using joy in this section to mean positive emotions. One way to think of joy is to consider this example: without knowing more information it is hard to tell if 79 degrees Fahrenheit is cool or warm. If you were working outside on an extremely hot day and then came inside where it was 79 degrees, it would feel cool to you. If you were outside working on a very cold day and stepped inside where it was 79 degrees, it would feel warm to you. So which is it, warm or cold? The answer is: *it depends*. The same is true for joy. Rather than thinking about joy as either on or off, hot or cold, in or out, I suggest you start to think of joy in terms of a continuum of joy, from slight to intense.

Not that long ago I visited a close friend in the hospital who was recovering from major surgery. By the look on his face, I could tell he was in pain. However, I could not tell how much pain he was in. I asked him how bad it hurt. He told me the pain was about a six out of ten and pointed to a chart on the wall. The chart had comical cartoon faces depicting various levels of pain, from zero, no pain, all the way to ten, unbearable pain. Six represented intense pain. I thought about that for a moment. Without a comparative pain scale, how would a doctor know what dosage of pain killer to administer? The chart made sense to me.

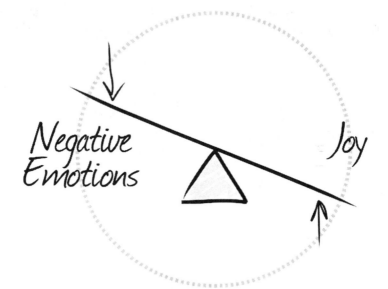

Now consider a similar chart for a joy scale that you will now use to communicate how you feel. When someone asks, "How ya doin'?" You could use the joy scale to say, "Today I am about a four hoping to be a five." I ask people all the time how they are, and I am surprised at how often someone tells me, "I am ok," or "I am fine," or "I am good." My typical response is, "You are only good? Not great?" Now, I am not foolish enough to think that every moment of every day will be positive and wonderful. Each day, every week, each month, year and decade can and will be filled with negative experiences. But we need to change the way we look at life and stop thinking that a day is good only if it is *all* good. You can have a good day and still have a tooth-ache. You can have a great day, even if you got stuck in traffic. You can have a joyful day even if you are not complimented, validated or recognized for something you have done.

Joy is available to be claimed right here, right now, right this moment. Joy is a powerful emotion that is felt along a continuum of positive emotions. If you cannot feel it, if you are not in-joy, then it is time to learn skills that will help you reduce negative emotions and intensify joy by creating positive emotions. The only other way to be in-joy is to wait for the right circumstances and events that bring joy to you. Don't wait for what brings you joy. Create it! Step into it. Feel it.

Chapter 26

What Does Joy Feel Like?

Most of my clients are adept at describing their negative emotions. I have found that to be true of most people. Thanks to the news, politics, modern psychology and other institutions, we are all well versed in the vocabulary of negative emotions. Think for a moment about the various conversations you have had over the past seven days. Chances are those conversations, whether with a co-worker, your family, a stranger or your spouse, were focused on what is wrong and not what is right. We have been trained to be negative. This training might have come from well-intentioned parents, managers, teachers or partners who felt they were doing us a favor by pointing out what is wrong. What are the results culturally? You don't have to look far to find that, as a society, we are preoccupied with feelings of depression, anxiety and fear.

For the first part of my career I had a job that required me to spend hours a day driving from one account to another. During that time I listened to a popular talk show by a prominent relationship therapist. This particular therapist was an expert in critical thinking. She prided herself in 'telling it like it is' and being straight with the people who were brave enough to call in. It wasn't long until I too was steeped in critical thinking and felt I was doing myself, my children, my wife and even my customers a favor by being 'keeping it real' and 'telling it like it is.' In reality, I wasn't doing anyone any favors, and rather than 'keeping it real,' I was keeping it negative. Don't be tempted into thinking it is in vogue to be negative, critical and 'tell it like it is.' I quickly learned that I was alienating the people I loved the most by 'keeping it real.' I was actually robbing my relationships of any chance of influencing them positively.

Our attachment to negativity is demonstrated by self-indictment, self-judging or being critical of others. These behaviors increase negative emotions that block your ability to experience the joy that is available to you. Joy is always present and can be felt if you give it a chance by reducing your negative emotions.

In essence there are only three ways for you to experience joy. First, you can simply wait for the right circumstances to come along. This is unpredictable, and chances are that you will be waiting a long time to feel joy. Let's face it, life is filled with negativity, and things just go wrong. If you just wait for things to go right, you will miss out on a lot of the joy that life has to offer you. The second way to feel joy every day is to learn how limit or reduce your negative emotions by overcoming joy blockers. Thirdly, you can create joy. Later in this section I will cover 10 ways to overcome those things that block joy. I will help you learn how to create joy and experience it every day.

There are just as many ways to express positive emotions as there are to express negative emotions, but we rarely use them. For instance, take the word love. It is often easier to define love by what it is not, rather than what it is. This is not because the words don't exist to describe love, but because we have not become used to the words or because they are simply uncommon. If a close friend or spouse says, "I love you," you instinctively know it is a different form of emotion than if they were to say, "I love this hamburger."

Just as there are different forms of love, there are different forms of and words to describe joy. Here are just a few you could use that express what joy feels like:

Blissful	Exhilarated	Spiritual
Cheerful	Exulting	Ignited
Delighted	Happy and happier	Excited

Inner warmth	Ecstatic	Pleased
Love	Euphoria	Peaceful
Gleeful	Jubilant	Enthused

I am not suggesting that the next time someone asks how you are doing that you answer, "Blissful, thank you." Unfortunately, you might get a strange look, and that person might think you had just taken a 'happy pill.' However, you might indeed be feeling just that. The question is not so much how to describe what you feel to others but how to create it within yourself and how to prevent it from disappearing.

Another aspect of joy is that we are typically more able to recognize it in others than we are in ourselves. It is unfortunate that we have been trained to minimize our own good feelings as a way of being considerate of those who may not be experiencing a great day. I was recently scheduled for a flight from Phoenix, Arizona to Chicago, Illinois that was cancelled. It was the first part of my journey, and the cancellation completely ruined my chances of getting to my final destination on time. I was inconvenienced but not devastated. Many of my fellow travelers were perplexed as to why I was not more upset, thinking that to be positive about the event minimized its seriousness. Don't fall into that kind of peer pressure. You can feel joy even when your flight is cancelled. Let me warn you against quickly dismissing what I just said. You can feel joy even when things don't go right and you are seriously inconvenienced. It is not the same level of joy you would feel at a party in your honor or falling in love for the first time, but you can still experience a degree of joy, nonetheless. It might be lower on the joy continuum, but we don't have to fall off the scale. We need to change our mindset from an all-or-nothing mentality of joy to realize that it is always available to us and has significant benefits. As you learn the skills in this section to reduce negative emotions and increase your positive emotions, you will experience being in-joy more often and reap the results. Following are some of the benefits you can experience:

More energy: People who are joyful or who are in-joy have more energy. Their energy comes from within and is felt by the people around them. This is not just energy to stay alert or to be more productive, which are great benefits in and of themselves but also energy that attracts positive people and can be felt when they enter a room. This energy can catalyze the joy of others as well, creating an overall feeling of well-being and emotions between two or more people.

Happiness and contentment: People who consider themselves as joyful have a higher degree of contentment with themselves and the world around them. They are not blind to the problems of the world and are not immune to bad things happening to them. They simply have a stronger internal coping mechanism that allows them to accept the world as it is, hope for it to be better and contribute positive change at a higher and more effective level.

Self-worth and self-esteem: There is an interesting cycle that begins with knowing your self-worth and working to increase it. As your self-worth increases, so does your joy. As your joy increases, your self-worth increases. That worthiness will be felt in every aspect of your life. Self-worth begets joy, which begets higher self-worth. It's a wonderful cycle to experience in your life.

Appropriate humility: The reason I call this appropriate humility is to distinguish it from self-pity. People who are in-joy are able to give credit where credit is due. As a young man I heard this quote, which I think of to this day, "There is no limit to what a man can do if he does not care who gets the credit." Joy begets love and love does not envy; neither is love jealous. Being appropriately humble will attract joyful people to you and actually open up opportunities for you to influence others for good.

Decreased need to complain: Joyful people are more tolerant of negative situations and the ups and downs of life. People who report feelings of joy complain less about physical and emotional ailments, change and mishaps.

Optimism: Joyfulness and optimism go hand in hand. Optimists are healthier, wealthier, are more likely to get a pay increase. They handle stress and change better, are more creative, have better jobs and live longer. Joyful people have the same characteristics and tend to experience the world in more positive terms.

Better health: Joy is associated with health. While some people believe that you will experience joy once you are healthier, it is actually the other way around. Joy contributes to a stronger immune system. You see, our physical and emotional states are interconnected. As you experience joy, you boost your immune system, which leads to better health. Better health leads to a greater ability to experience joy, and so the cycle continues. If you are experiencing poor health, give serious consideration to developing skills that produce joy, and it will greatly improve your health.

I AM STRONG!

Chapter 27

Joy Inhibitors

Let me reiterate that joy is not an emotion that is turned on or off; it is something that is always available to you and can be experienced at any time. In this regard it is like the sun. The sun shines every day. There is never a day without sunshine, and if you climb to a high enough altitude you can experience the constant warmth of the sun. Though the sun is shining, you may not be able to see it or feel it because of clouds or other obstacles blocking the sun. If you are not feeling joy at this moment it is likely due to emotional clouds blocking it. As a young boy I grew up in Southern California only thirty minutes from the beach. In early summer it was often cloudy at the beach until either the wind blew the clouds away or the sun warmed enough to dissipate the cloud cover. Though we have little control over clouds at the beach, we do have control over the emotional clouds that block our ability to experience joy. In many cases these joy-blockers have become a way of life and have been around so long we hardly consider them as joy-blockers, but rather, just as the way things are. With a few refinements and minor changes, you will see that you can begin to experience joy and reap the benefits I discussed earlier in this section. Let's discuss some of these joy-blockers:

Being too busy: Are you burning the proverbial candle at both ends? Are you running here and there trying to get too many things done? Are you feeling the pressure of work, family and social obligations? I have met far too many clients who emotionally crash and burn, only to recover and start the whole rat race over again. They are so busy that they are not only frequently or perpetually stressed but also are unable to experience the simple wonders of life, let alone the joy that is available to them.

Physical and mental clutter: Your physical surroundings can have a direct impact on your ability to experience joy. If your work desk, bedroom, closet, kitchen and car are full of clutter, you are limiting the joy you can experience. Even as a young man I was aware that clutter causes me anxiety. Not that I am a neat-freak, but clutter causes me to feel more stress than when my work area, bedroom and other places are not cluttered. The same is true of our mind and emotions. This is about more than being too busy; this is about trying to juggle too many balls at once and feeling like you are not doing well at any of them. If this is you, it is time to objectively prioritize what you are thinking about, what you are doing and de-clutter physically and mentally.

Mind-numbing distractions: With our lives being so busy and so cluttered, it is quite tempting to veg-out in front of the TV, mindlessly surf the internet, and immerse ourselves in video games, on-line poker or social media. While all of those distractions are not inherently bad or wrong and can provide some pleasure, they can consume too much of our time and can also be a negative distraction. For instance, watching the news just before you retire for the night can create more stress. Getting caught up in social media drama can also create more anxiety. With all of these distractions it is good to have a healthy amount of self-awareness to determine if they are adding to your stress, preventing you from experiencing joy, or keeping you from doing things that are more constructive and emotionally rewarding.

Emotional bad habits: We all have emotional habits, which include how we react in certain situations, how we judge others, and how we let others push our 'buttons.' Most, if not all, of these emotional bad habits are just that: habits. By habits, I mean they are learned behaviors that often prevent us from experiencing joy. For example, anger, insecurity, low self-worth and many other things I have covered in the earlier sections can be joy blockers. Fortunately, it is within our power to change our habits.

Unhealthy preoccupation with the past or the future: Now-time is quality time. As discussed in an earlier section, it is time to learn how to unload your baggage from the past. The present is often contaminated by our past or unhealthy anticipation of the future. You can be a hero and no longer be a victim to your past. Your future is yet to be defined. You will have a much brighter future as you learn to experience joy in the present. You don't need to wait to have the perfect house, spouse, job or car to experience joy. You can experience it right now!

Fear, uncertainly and doubt: Fear, uncertainty and doubt are close cousins that feed off of one another. They not only block your ability to experience joy but also your ability to be happy and experience love. Fear and joy cannot exist together at the same time. Now, you may think you can compartmentalize your fear, thinking that fear of being laid-off has nothing to do with nor will impact the joy you can experience at home. But you are fooling yourself. Fear in any aspect of your life will diminish your ability to experience joy. Like fear, uncertainty and doubt also diminish your ability to experience joy. The uncertainty and doubt I refer to here is about your ability to feel self-worth and self-confidence. This kind of uncertainty leads to doubt. There is much uncertainty in life; however, you can have uncertainty about life but still feel confident that it will all work out. It is uncertainty and doubt without faith that prevents experiencing joy.

Resentment and unwillingness to forgive: As you can tell and as you might expect, experiencing joy requires internal and emotional freedom. Resentment which stems from an unwillingness to forgive creates emotional slavery. You actually become a slave to your own negative emotion. Resentment and joy cannot exist together at the same time. If you resent someone, something or even yourself, it is time to release yourself from this bondage. If you are still struggling with this, please go back and study Part 3, "The Miracles of Authentic Forgiving." I find that I constantly need to remind myself to forgive. I try my best to recognize feelings of resentment and use that awareness to trigger forgiveness. Sometimes resentment can trick us into thinking it is a good feeling; resentment tells us it is our right to level the playing field to make things fair. But don't believe the lie. If you feel resentment, you can't experience joy and you need to forgive.

Living without purpose: When we are living a life without purpose it affects every aspect of our life. We are more prone to depression, we are more indecisive, we can feel lonely and it can also lower our feelings of self-worth. If you still feel you don't have a purpose, please go back and review the previous section. When you are living your true life purpose you open yourself up to experience joy more fully and more regularly.

Internal programming: If we allow it, the way we were raised by our parents and our previous life experiences can have a dramatic impact on how we experience joy. I recently met with a client who described her childhood as an 'intellectual' experience. In other words, her parents undervalued emotion and underscored the cerebral. When that happens we grow up thinking that's the way things are. You can overcome your internal programming and even your own emotional DNA by learning and applying the skills presented in this book. As you do you will be amazed at the joy you will experience.

Chapter 28

Creating Joy

You have learned that there are really only three ways to experience joy: waiting for joy to just happen; reducing negative emotions, thereby reducing or eliminating what inhibits our ability to experience joy; and by actually creating joy, making it happen. Let me now share with you several practical ways to reduce negativity and create positive emotions.

Enjoy the Touch and Feel of Gratitude: Gratitude is an important ingredient to feeling optimistic, overcoming your adversity and experiencing joy. Studies have shown that purposeful gratitude can help us overcome diseases, such as cancer. It can reduce the effect of other types of personal setbacks.[20] In many studies researchers have been able to measure that something as simple as counting your blessings can boost your positive emotions for as long as two weeks. What is interesting about these studies is that they also show that we quickly adapt to our own feelings of gratitude. If we count the same blessings over and over again, we rapidly become bored with the task, and the positive emotions begin to fade after about two weeks. Here is an example of what I mean: have you ever been without hot water? This recently happened to our family when our hot water heater went out and needed replacement. For almost three weeks we were forced to use cold water for bathing and washing. When the repairs were finally finished and we once again had hot water, we felt so grateful. The intense gratitude of having hot water again disappeared in just a few days as we adapted and fell back into full expectation that we would have hot water each time we opened the hot water faucet.

To overcome this powerful adaptation to our blessings, I recommend training yourself to feel gratitude for all the things that add to the value and quality of your life. I call this the "touch and feel" of gratitude. You can train yourself to feel gratitude by saying thanks for everything you physically touch that you feel grateful for. For instance, each time you pick up your mobile phone you can say to yourself, "I am so grateful to have this phone." When you touch your car keys, the door to your house, sit in your chair at the office, hug your wife, hug your children, or eat a meal, all you have to do is start saying to yourself how grateful you are. This creates a habit of gratitude that overcomes the problem of becoming bored with it, and it will intensify your feelings of thankfulness.

Gratitude, especially purposeful gratitude, gratitude that you have trained yourself to feel and experience, creates the positive emotions that will boost your ability to feel joy on a regular basis.

Practical Tip:

A good way to get into the 'touch and feel' of gratitude is to color code your thankfulness. Pick a color. It doesn't matter what color it is as long as your remember it throughout the day. Then each time you see that color, take a moment to express gratitude for whatever you happen to be touching.

Live Drama Free: No one is immune to drama. The drama in our lives can come from work, family, friends, health and even the news. In almost every speaking engagement, I can visibly see the audience perk up when I start to talk about how to live drama free. In many cases drama is created when someone wants us to share the responsibility for their urgent issues, their problems, and even their irresponsibility. The antidote to this kind of drama is to underreact. Learning to underreact is such an important principle that in my previous book, *The Happiness Factor: How to Be Happy No Matter What!*, I dedicate an entire chapter on how to it.

Underreact is the opposite of 'freaking out'! I am sure you all know someone who freaks out, and it is quite likely that if you are reading this book, you are the one who freaks out. Let me tell you something about freaking out – if you are the one who freaks out, you are likely not being getting the whole truth in your relationships. Think about it, if you know so-and-so freaks out, and you have something important and urgent to tell him, most likely you change the story, reduce the importance, or leave out parts of the story so that they don't freak out—you don't give the whole truth. This is particularly true at home. If your children see you as someone who freaks out all the time, your children will keep things from you. You will know of the little stuff, the meaningless stuff, but not the big or important things that your children are facing. Underreacting does not diminish the seriousness or the importance of an issue; it is more about being able to respond more appropriately and to be at your best when something significant needs your attention.

Let me illustrate by telling you a personal story. It was a Friday night at 11:30 p.m., and I was getting ready to go to bed when the phone rang. My wife answered the phone, and I could tell immediately that something was wrong. Within a few seconds my wife brought the telephone to me explaining in an urgent tone, "It's Taylor (our 23 year-old-son). His car has broken down on the interstate about 20 miles away and needs you to come get him." Now, I don't know about you, but 11:30 p.m. is my upper limit on a Friday night, and the last thing I wanted to do was tow my son's car in the middle of the night. The instant I heard what the problem was, I started to calculate how long it would take. Well, I didn't have a tow rope, nor did I have a truck to tow a car. I would have to borrow a truck, buy a tow rope or a chain, which alone would take until after midnight.

Then I'd have to travel the 20 miles to where my son was, hook up the car, tow it back and return the truck! Needless to say I was about to freak out! Not so much that it was an insurmountable task, but it would turn out to be a major inconvenience, and above all, I needed my sleep! Perhaps things like this happen to you all the time. Maybe it is not your son but your boss who does this to you, or maybe it's your brother or sister. I could feel the drama increase as I contemplated having to go get my son. However, I had been trying to truly practice what I preach, and so I decided to put *underreact* to the test.

Practical Tip:

Here is a three-step process to underreact and reduce the drama in your life:

1. **Say out loud, "I choose to underreact."** This is an important first step, as it signals to the people around you that you are not going to freak out. It also serves as an emotional trigger to yourself that you are not going to engage in the drama.
2. **Take a step back.** Literally take a step backwards if you can. Although this is a physical act, it signals an emotional response that you are actually stepping away from the situation.
3. **Take a deep breath and let it out.** This has a calming effect and helps you construct a more appropriate response.

I know that when I freak out I don't make the best decisions, and for many of you it is the same. When we are emotionally engaged, we tend to lose our objectivity and make rash decisions. By following the three-step process to underreact, you will actually give a more appropriate response, and in many cases the problem will seem smaller and may even solve itself. Let me demonstrate by continuing the story of my Friday night drama. I told my wife, "I choose to underreact," something she is now used to hearing me say. In fact, all of my family is used to me saying that, and I have even heard others who know me say it as well. I took a step back and inhaled a deep breath, and in that moment the problem solved itself. Because I had chosen to underreact, I was able to recall that I had purchased roadside assistance for my son. He had a cell phone, he had the number in his glove-box, and all HE had to do was call the number and get a tow. By the time he got home, I was fast asleep without any drama.

When you start to practice this in real life situations, you are more at your best and able to act with more objectivity; in many cases you will think of a solution to a problem that would not have come to you had you freaked out. It takes a bit of practice. As you practice this, you will no longer be thought of as the one who freaks out, and you will train others to underreact as well. The benefit to this is that as you reduce the drama in your life, you reduce negative emotions and increase your ability to experience joy.

Accentuate the Positive – Eliminate the Negative: Many of the people I speak to believe that an experience or a situation is not positive unless all aspects of the experience are positive. Although we had other things to discuss, Veronica insisted that we talk about her recent visit with her daughter, Sarah, who was about to turn 30. Veronica and her daughter have had an on-again, off-again relationship for most of Sarah's life. When I asked how the visit went, Veronica went on and on about how bad the visit had turned out and bemoaned that she and her daughter could not have a positive and constructive relationship. Wanting to know more, I asked Veronica to play out the visit for me so I could get a feel for how it went. As I suspected, the visit was mostly positive. They had a great conversation and enjoyed their time together. They had laughed and seemed to enjoy each other's company. At some point, near the middle of the visit, Veronica brought up the subject of day-care. Veronica didn't like the fact that Sarah put her children in day-care a few days a week even though Sarah was not working. Sarah took the question as a criticism, and for a few moments the conversation went negative. Once the subject changed to something more positive the visit continued more positively and ended quite well. At least to me it ended well. Veronica could not get over the few moments of tension when she asked Sarah about day-care. For Veronica, the visit with her daughter could only be considered a positive experience if the entire visit was positive. Veronica had an all-or-nothing mentality about most experiences, and because most experiences are seldom 100% positive, she seldom felt joy.

What about you? Do you, too, have an all-or-nothing mentality about your experiences? If so, you may be missing out on a tremendous amount of joy that already exists in your life. You are missing it because, like Veronica, you are focused on the negative, rather than the positive. You can change this by lowering your positive experience set point. Rather than maintaining an all-or-nothing mentality, simply turn your focus to all that is or was positive in an experience and focus on that. If Veronica simply disregarded the short conversation about day-care, she would realize that she has a better than average relationship with her daughter, and she would be able to feel joy in that relationship. We all have a tendency to accentuate the negative to the point of overshadowing the positive things in our life. By lowering your positive experience set point, you will increase the amount of positive emotions that come into your life on a daily basis. This same approach was popularized in a 1944 song with lyrics by Johnny Mercer. The song, "Ac-Cent-Tchu-Ate the Positive" was written after Johnny Mercer attended a sermon on the subject and thought the words were colorful enough to set to music.[21] The lyrics are appropriate here to make the point about lowering your positive experience set point by eliminating the negative:

> You've got to accentuate the positive,
> Eliminate the negative,
> And latch on to the affirmative;
> Don't mess with Mister In-Between.

You've got to spread joy up to the maximum,
Bring gloom down to the minimum,
Have faith or Pandemonium's
Liable to walk upon the scene.

If you want to increase the amount of joy you experience, it is critical that you follow the advice of this song: accentuate the positive, eliminate the negative, bring gloom down to the minimum, and don't mess with Mister In-Between. One of the best ways to lower your positive experience set point is to simply be more objective about your experiences. As a young adult I would often speak of my childhood as a very negative experience. It wasn't until later in life I realized that I was doing myself, my father and my family a disservice. My childhood was not all negative, and it was not all positive. When I finally changed my focus to eliminate the negative (see Part 4: From Victim to Hero in 90 Seconds), my joy increased tremendously and the same can happen for you. This does not mean that the negative things aren't important or should not be addressed. It is simply a matter of putting them in proper perspective. There is a huge difference between things being all negative versus things being part negative and part positive. If you want to experience more joy in your life, you can start immediately by doing these two things: accentuating the positive in any and all experiences and eliminating your all-or-nothing mentality.

Practical Tip:

You may think that accentuating the positive is a little corny or immature. I assure you, it is not. Besides, the only thing you have to lose is your negative attitude. If you want to experience more joy, it is time you lost that anyway.

❭ Recognize that very few situations are all negative or all positive, and focus on the positive.

❭ Learn to disregard the negative unless you absolutely have to acknowledge it.

❭ Prioritize being at peace over being right.

❭ Practice retelling the story you tell yourself about what has happened to you, as was described in Part 4.

❭ Withdraw from negative conversations; don't let them draw you in and cloud your vision.

❭ Savor past positive experiences.

Develop Emotional Generosity: Unfortunately, our joy is often spoiled by the people around us. Whether intentionally or accidentally, people, their words and deeds can spoil the best of days and suck the joy right out of it. If you are surrounded by people who are negative, critical, or emotional bullies you may be tempted to simply withdraw from those people in order to experience joy. That may work for a short period until other negative people enter your life. No matter where you go, even in your own mind, you will always encounter negativity from other people. The better approach is to learn skills to maintain or increase your level of joy, even when you experience negativity from others. One such skill is emotional generosity. The term 'emotional generosity' was used by Reverend Scott W. Alexander in one of his sermons. He says, "Emotional generosity is the quality of being kind and welcoming and understanding of persons around you…in all of their limitations, imperfections and flaws. Emotional generosity means that you give other human beings the benefit of the doubt, that you cut them some slack, and that you are slow to be harsh, condemning or judgmental."[22]

However, the act of emotional generosity does not mean that you are going to let someone off the hook. It does not mean that they are not accountable for their actions or that withdrawing your association isn't eventually appropriate, especially after multiple attempts have failed to improve the atmosphere or safety within the relationship. But even in that case, emotional generosity can help us forgive and heal. While at first blush you may think emotional generosity means you are making an excuse for someone's misbehavior, it is really an act of compassion and understanding. It simply means that you are going to choose not to let another person rob you of joy. Emotional generosity is a sincere act of giving of who you are, not just of what you have. You are truly choosing to take the high road and by doing so you will see things more clearly.

Emotional generosity is so important that it is a skill covered in almost every section of this book. It takes some practice but can quickly be learned. Here is an example of how this can help you. I have a good friend whom I will call Dean. As Dean was growing up, his father was considered mean. His father was quick to anger and seldom complimented or praised Dean. Dean grew up reluctant to have friends over because he anticipated that his father would embarrass him by raising his voice or being gruff with his friends. Dean's mother was sympathetic but had grown to accept his father as grumpy and ornery. Dean grew to accept his father in the way his mother had, but it still bothered him and caused him pain as he remembered his childhood. As Dean approached his 37th birthday, he got the news that doctors had found a slow-growing tumor in his father's brain. The tumor had probably been growing since Dean's father was a young man. Fortunately, the tumor was successfully removed with almost no impact on brain function. However, there was a significant difference in his father's demeanor. From the moment he woke from the anesthesia, Dean's father was a different man. He was no longer an ogre seeing the bad in everything. Dean's father became a kinder, gentler, more affectionate man. Dean was able to finally experience the father he had always dreamed of having. Would it have made a difference if Dean was aware as a young boy that is father had a tumor that caused him to be grumpy? I think it would have.

Now consider that when someone is negative, critical, selfish, demanding, angry or jealous, that they too may have something causing this misbehavior. Putting it in these terms, it is easier to give them the benefit of the doubt, to cut them some slack and even look upon them with compassion instead of anger. As you become emotionally generous you become a compassionate participant instead of an argumentative contender.

Emotional generosity does more for you than it does for the other person. When you become generous with your emotions, you get more joy in return. You eliminate negativity from other people. I am fortunate to have learned this lesson from my own daughter. She is naturally emotionally generous. If I share some complaint with her about another person, she is quick to give them the benefit of the doubt with soothing and calming words such as, "I am sure that if they knew better they would have acted better, " or "I am sure they're having an off day because that doesn't sound like them." We too can develop this same ability to give the benefit of the doubt or cut some slack and increase our joy by decreasing the negative emotions in dealing with the misbehavior of others.

Practical Tip:

Emotional generosity is when you give of who you are, not just what you have. This means you will give someone, including yourself, the benefit of the doubt and cut some slack.

> Express appreciation. Don't be afraid to tell someone they have done a good job and to compliment them sincerely.

> Let others speak. In a conversation try to truly listen to what others are saying. You will be surprised at how much positive energy there will be as you listen instead of preoccupy your mind with what you're going to say. Don't just wait to speak; listen.

> Stop comparing yourself to others. Think of a person you hold in high regard and respect. Now consider that you are equal to them. They may have more experience or talents, but that does not make them more important than you.

> Stop trying to impress others. You don't need to impress anyone. In Part 1 you have learned how to increase your self-worth. As your worth grows, your need to impress will disappear.

Sit Down and Shut Up: Life is busy and it is easy to become inundated with text messages, voicemail, email, conference calls, soccer, and ballet to the point that we don't even slow down when we eat. Even in the car, where just a few years ago we only had the radio to contend with, we now have constant communication to keep us occupied. It is as if we are in an 'on' state 24 hours a day. We quickly understand that if we don't charge our cell phone it will run out of battery and won't function, yet we are reluctant to apply the same principle to ourselves. As our emotional batteries run down, we become hypersensitive to stress, disease and negativity. It impairs our ability to feel joy at a deep and powerful level. When that happens we receive only momentary episodes of joy that are fleeting and superficial.

Elizabeth came to me saying that her life was out of control. She felt unable to deal with life's daily stresses, she needed to find a new job and a new place to live, and she struggled with challenges associated with her nearly-adult children. Within in a short period of time I learned that Elizabeth loved to read. She had interests in diverse subjects and would often be in the middle of at least four different books. Reading brought her peace and helped her feel grounded, and if nothing else, she had accomplished something that day. Her reading was more like a devotional that included time to think and meditate. It all went to pieces when she lost her job. The first thing to go was her reading and meditation, as the stress of finding a new job became unbearable.

The first thing I suggested to Elizabeth was that she get back into the habit of reading. I encouraged her to pick something light and easy to read to get started. She was reluctant at first, remarking that she needed to spend every waking hour searching for a job. I cautioned her against becoming obsessed with finding a job and suggested she take time to recharge her batteries and create some structure to her life that was now missing after losing her job. In our next session seven days later, I could see the remarkable difference in her countenance. It was clear that the reading had worked and that she felt more able to tackle her other obstacles to feeling great joy.

While it is not always that simple, it is almost always that remarkable. One way to start is to learn the art of SDASU –to sit down and shut up. Although I have always known about this principle, I was pleased to find it referred to in the book *Super Joy* written by Paul Pearsall, Ph.D.[23] While I don't typically use the words 'shut up,' I think they are appropriate here to raise your awareness to take the time to relax, be still and clear your mind.

Applying the Art of SDASU

Raise your tolerance for silence. We have a tendency to fill each moment with talking, texting or music. I often pause in my coaching sessions to assess how comfortable a client is with silence. Most often they are not, and each time I pause, it is taken as a cue for them to start talking again. While I want a client to do most of the talking, I also want to gauge their comfort with just sitting there in quiet. You don't have to fill silence with endless banter. Even at a business lunch or office dinner, you don't have to be talking all the time. If the conversation hits a lull, just wait. Next time you are in the car, turn off your cell phone, turn off the radio or CD player and just drive in silence. This will increase your tolerance for silence and also raise your comfort. This becomes especially true with teenagers. I made it a practice to never go anywhere alone when my children were living at home. What drove them crazy is that when they were in the car, I would not turn on the radio. It only took a few miles before they started to fill the void with talking. I heard things in the car that I probably would have never heard otherwise.

Practical Tip:

I recommend at least 15 minutes of silence a day with a strong recommendation that you increase it to 30 minutes as soon as you can. This will ground you and center you from the inside out and increase your ability to experience joy.

Raise your tolerance for being alone. I have found that the majority of my clients live with a minor conflict. The conflict is created by a strong desire for peace and quiet, while at the same time they are uncomfortable being alone. My recommendation of 15 to 30 minutes of silence each day is combined with a recommendation that you become more comfortable being alone. We are surrounded by people, noise and activity. To experience more joy in your life, we need to extract ourselves from the hustle and bustle of daily living and spend some alone time. This will enable you to feel more comfortable with yourself without the expectations of others. You don't have to be in silence when you are alone, although you may very well want to be. Most of us have been taught that to be alone is less sociable and loners are not popular. Resist that thinking. Being alone, when done in moderation, is quite helpful.

Practical Tip:

Here are a few things you can do to increase your tolerance for being alone:

> Eat your lunch by yourself in a quiet place.

> Go to a movie alone.

> Drive alone somewhere other than just to and from work.

> Take time to just be with yourself.

Raise your tolerance for doing nothing. I love the bumper sticker that reads, "Don't just do something, sit there!" Admittedly when I saw this bumper sticker, it was on the back of a VW van at the beach. But it still struck me as good advice. I would not dare give this advice to a slacker. But I would bet that if you have made it this far in this book it's at least partly because you are not a slacker! So I feel comfortable recommending that you learn to sit still and do nothing. We were all raised to think that doing nothing is laziness, and while that is true in the extreme, doing nothing for a brief period each day helps you create a new perspective on things.

Practical Tip:

Take a few minutes each day to do nothing. For instance, when you are in line at Starbucks, don't pull out your cell phone to text someone or pretend to be busy. Just stand there and notice your surroundings and the other people around you. When you first get home from work, don't just jump in right away from one task to another, take a few minutes to just sit there and do nothing.

Learn to be comfortable with yourself. The three recommendations above, to raise your tolerance of silence, being alone and doing nothing, are all preparatory to becoming more comfortable with yourself. This means accepting yourself for who you are, what you have done, your goals and your aspirations. Some people refer to this as being comfortable in your own skin. This is a key to learning the art of SDASU. If you are not comfortable with yourself, you will find it difficult to sit alone in silence and do nothing. Your discomfort will cause you to reject my recommendations as foolishness. Recognize your discomfort as a sign that the reason you reject SDASU is because you find it hard to be alone with yourself. Whatever the reason – maybe you find it hard to sit still, maybe you need to be surrounded by people or maybe you just need to be validated. If that is the case, I recommend you return to Part 1 and work on the principles regarding how to increase your self-worth and self-confidence. If you are someone who needs others to be around you in order for you to feel important or simply to feel joy, you are dependent on those people or the situation in order to feel joy. In that case your joy will be minimized, and you will constantly be seeking out company or validation. Learn to trust and feel safe with yourself.

Practical Tip:

The next time you are in front of a mirror, linger there a bit longer and take a good look at yourself. Try to take in the details of your face, your hair, your skin. Look deep into your own eyes. For most people this is uncomfortable, but stay there and look at yourself as long as you can. Try to increase the amount of time you look at yourself each day. Soon you will be more comfortable with yourself.

Learning SDASU can have a profound impact on your ability to experience joy. You will also find you have a greater ability to cope with adversity and change. Negativity will have less impact on you, and you will experience more balance in your life.

Overcome P.O.D. – Problem Obsession Disorder. I often have a client who comes to me for help to solve a major problem. This problem, this issue, this obstacle has become their life. They have become so fixated on this one problem that nothing else matters. They are so consumed with it that even the simple pleasures in life are foregone in order to avoid any distractions from solving the problem. Not that long ago a couple came to me for help dealing with their son who was addicted to heroin. I will call them Sam and Julie. Sam insisted they come to me, not so much to help them deal with their son's addiction, but as Sam put it, to help Julie break her addiction to saving their son from his addiction. In the first session it became quite clear to me why Sam was concerned. Julie had become obsessed to the point that she had quit her job and spent an enormous amount of time researching heroin addiction and possible treatments. Her reasoning was quite sound; she felt compelled to do all she could to 'save' her son. Sam was just as concerned but had a more balanced approach. Julie had stopped cooking, stopped cleaning and even had reduced her own self-care to a minimum. She stopped doing her hair, stopped wearing makeup and, according to Sam, seldom got out of her pajamas unless she was going to an Al-Anon meeting or visiting a rehab facility. Julie was in the throes of P.O.D. – Problem Obsession Disorder – and was losing her ability to be effective in helping their son. Once I understood the situation, my next question surprised Julie and almost caused her to leave. I asked, "Does your son want help?" Her answer was a simple and tear-filled, "No."

Herman Melville in the classic book Moby Dick artfully describes a similar situation with the book's main character that has since become known as Captain Ahab Syndrome. You will recall in this book that the vengeful Captain Ahab is obsessed with capturing the white whale named Moby Dick. Captain Ahab Syndrome is characterized by a complete obsession with a problem or obstacle to the point that nothing else mattered. This is typified by a scene midway through the book when, out of frustration, Captain Ahab throws his last life's pleasure, his pipe, overboard. Julie had taken on a whale of a problem that was literally sucking the life out of her and depriving her of life's pleasure and joy. She justified her actions with good intentions of saving her son, a son who didn't want to be saved. Like Captain Ahab, we all have a whale of a problem to deal with. What is your 'white whale'? What is that one aspect of your life that controls all you do and feel? It could be your job, parenting, being a caretaker, grief, pain, any sort of thing. Like the good captain, you may have become tied to this whale for so long that it has become your own version of normal. Life doesn't have to be that way. It is time to let go and let joy into your life.

I have met wonderful people who have spent years totally dedicated to taking care of an elderly parent. When that parent finally passes, they are lost and fall deep into depression, as if their only reason to live has suddenly been taken from them. There is more to life than the problem you are experiencing. It is time to come up for air, to live life and to pursue the problem with moderation. Certainly there are times when an urgent and dedicated response is needed, but don't let it become your life. Another client, Andrea had been divorced for more than three years. Her primary goal in life had become to make her ex-husband's life miserable. She would phone him late at night asking where he had been and who he had been with. She would plot elaborate plans to embarrass him in front of his family, friends and girlfriends. Andrea was hurt and still felt the pain of the messy divorce. Her life was filled with anger toward her husband. She was obsessed and needed real help to overcome her obsession so she could feel joy again.

If this describes you then I suggest you seek help. Don't let this one thing get in the way of you experiencing joy. Joy is too valuable, too precious to let it slip away. Joy is here and now.

Practical Tip:

Here are six ways to overcome P.O.D.:

❯ Talk tenderly to yourself. Engage in positive self-talk to keep from spiraling down into depression.

❯ Surrender your problem to God or your higher power. Try to recognize what you can control and what you cannot.

❯ Try to look objectively at what the worst thing that could happen would be. Unless this is a life or death situation, you can relax a bit. This does make it less serious but you will be able to cope better when you are not as involved.

❯ Create distance: try to withdraw from the problem if you can. Distance may reduce the intensity.

❯ Underreact. Try to become an underreact-expert to keep from freaking out.

❯ Seek help. If you still cannot overcome your obsession with a problem, it may be time to seek help.

I AM STRONG!

True joy is not something that comes to us when the circumstances are just right, when we are at our best, or when the stars align. Joy is here and now. If you can't feel joy it is because something is blocking it. I am confident that the principles in this section will help you break down your obstacles to experiencing joy so you can feel the great warmth, love, and power that joy can bring into to your life.

Do you have P.O.D. –
Problem Obsession Disorder?

Using the scale of 1 (Disagree) to 10 (Agree) answer the following questions:

1	I think about the same problem every day all day long.
	Disagree 1 2 3 4 5 6 7 8 9 10 Agree

2	Even when I am busy doing other things this problem is not far from my mind.
	Disagree 1 2 3 4 5 6 7 8 9 10 Agree

3	Do you consider this problem larger than life itself and something you must resolve although it seems unsolvable?
	Disagree 1 2 3 4 5 6 7 8 9 10 Agree

4	Do you believe you own this problem? That it is yours, and yours alone?
	Disagree 1 2 3 4 5 6 7 8 9 10 Agree

5	Do you feel that if this problem were gone you would have nothing to live for?
	Disagree 1 2 3 4 5 6 7 8 9 10 Agree

6	Does it seem like the world is against you? That when you get close to solving this problem something happens to prevent you from solving it?
	Disagree 1 2 3 4 5 6 7 8 9 10 Agree

7	Is your life defined in terms of this problem? Do you alter plans or activities because of this problem?
	Disagree 1 2 3 4 5 6 7 8 9 10 Agree

8	Have you put career, family, personal plans on hold because of this problem?
	Disagree 1 2 3 4 5 6 7 8 9 10 Agree

9	Does your life revolve around this problem to the extent that every song, every movie, every book or joke reminds you of your problem?											
	Disagree	1	2	3	4	5	6	7	8	9	10	Agree
10	Do you dream and daydream about this problem and find it hard to explain the nature of the problem to others?											
	Disagree	1	2	3	4	5	6	7	8	9	10	Agree

Add up the total score from the 10 questions: _____

A score of 50 or less means you likely have healthy view of any issues or problems you are facing.

A score of 50 or above indicates that you are facing a problem or issue that should be addressed before you can experience deeper and more meaningful joy.

I AM STRONG!

Part 7

Putting It All Together

Throughout this book are several suggestions on how to apply the skills and principles covered in each section. Here are several additional skills and principles that will help you realize your amazing worth, unload emotional baggage, discover your true life purpose and experience joy and happiness at some level each and every day.

1. Shift from knowing to learning – be curious.

Contention is created when we pre-judge another person, their attitude, their opinion and their actions. When you take a learning stance, rather than a position of judging, you can open yourself up to positive emotions that will bolster your self-esteem, make it easier to forgive and help you experience greater joy. When we think we are right or have a need to be right, it closes us off to learning and damages our relationships. Learn to be curious by asking simple questions of others:

- What are your thoughts on the subject?
- Am I seeing this correctly?
- How would you handle this?
- What advice do you have?

2. Prioritize blessing the lives of others.

Serving and blessing the life of another person benefits you in so many ways. It helps you put your adversity into perspective, helps you feel meaning and significance and raises your self-worth. This can take the form of a smile, a kind gesture or an act of kindness. Your intention is more important than what you do. If you were to make it a priority to bless the lives of everyone you encounter on a daily basis you will start to experience joy more frequently and abundantly.

3. Develop a thick skin and don't take things personally.

Taking offense comes at a price. The price you pay is reducing or eliminating positive emotions you could have experienced. Instead, you experience contention and negative emotions. Developing a thick skin does not mean that you should become submissive and let people walk all over you. It means that you don't take things personally. You handle the situation in a mature and open manner. It will be easier to have a thick skin as you increase your self-worth. This prevents current situations from becoming bad past experiences.

4.   Create a joy journal – savor the feeling of joy.

When things go bad, when we are feeling depressed or anxious, it is hard to mentally recall times when we experienced joy. However, savoring the feeling of joy you felt in the past is a quick antidote to depression. Keep a joy journal. Write down your feelings of joy and include when and how it happened. This helps you recall the feelings associated with joy and will help you get out of a rut. If you experience joy, write it down as soon as you can.

5.   Become a compassionate participant.

Whenever you hear gossip or criticism of a person who is not present, do your best to stand up for them. Become compassionate about the person being criticized and stop to think how much you would want someone to stick up for you. Be that person. It will change the moment and give you an opportunity to be a hero in someone's life.

6.   Become an observer – even a self-observer.

Begin to think of yourself as an innocent bystander. All too often we can get caught up in office gossip and the negative emotions of others and take on their contention. If you can be just an observer you will not allow your emotions to be impacted. You can maintain a high degree of positive emotions, even when there is negativity around you. Also, learn how to be a self-observer. This will allow you to become more aware of your thoughts, actions and feelings. The more aware you are, the more you can experience the benefits of I AM STRONG.

7. Trust yourself and follow your intuition.

Often we create our own anxiety because we are feeling one way but act another. Pay attention to your intuition, your gut feelings, and trust them more. When you do this you will feel more congruent and live with greater integrity. This eliminates much of the anxiety we feel and opens us up to trust in ourselves and believe that we make a difference.

8. Breathe.

You would be surprised at how much we hold our breath during the day, as if we suffer from waking apnea. Breathing, while mostly an unconscious action, should become more conscious and purposeful. Breathing exercises can reduce tension, increase energy and healing, as well as provide a calming effect to reduce negative emotions.

9. Meditate.

There are many forms of meditation, including simply sitting still and focusing your mind, advanced forms of meditation for long periods of time, and moving meditations like Tai Chi. I recommend learning some form of meditation as a way of learning how to still your mind and your body. This helps you put things in perspective, allows you to be in tune with yourself and reduces stress.

10. Stand taller.

Our posture is typically a reflection of our emotions. If you want to feel more energetic and happier, practice standing with greater poise and walking with purpose. As you stand taller, take a deep breath as well. You will feel momentarily rejuvenated and energized. When you stand taller (even just sitting straighter) people react to you differently – they treat you more positively and with more respect.

11. Under-think – stop over-thinking.

Rumination is another way to reduce the joy we can experience.

Ruminating is over-thinking. When you are thinking about something to the point of not thinking about anything else, you can create a negative spiral of thoughts that typically ends in depression or anxiety. Learn to under-think. That means that if no solution to your problem is apparent, stop thinking about it. You will be surprised at how many solutions come to you when you are not thinking about the problem itself.

12.   Visualize and savor joy.

Create a scene in your mind of what it feels like to experience the joy you seek. Make this an elaborate scene using as many of your senses as possible. Be imaginative and make it memorable. This is a scene you will rehearse in your mind over and over again to remind you of what it feels like to experience joy. The more you practice, the more joy you bring into your present experience. This is not about remembering a time when you felt joy but a visual exercise of what it means to feel joy right now.

13.   Replace 'I can't' with 'I haven't.'

How many times do you say 'I can't' when you actually mean 'I haven't'? The word 'can't' almost always creates internal contention. For instance, if someone asks if you play the piano, instead of saying 'I can't,' you can say 'I haven't learned yet.' This is a more positive expression of your ability to learn the piano if you put your mind to it. This will create a support system for a healthy self-worth, enable you to forgive easier and helps you discover your true life's purpose.

14.   Don't resist self-care.

We need to find a balance between caring for others and caring for ourselves. There is an old adage that says "you cannot give what you do not have." Take the time to care for yourself. This is not selfishness, and this is not being self-centered. This is about rejuvenating your heart, mind and emotions so that you can experience joy without obstacles to prevent it.

15.   Smile – smile a lot!

Studies have shown that a smile creates a chemical change in both the giver and the receiver. Even if you don't feel like it, learn to smile at everyone you encounter. You will be amazed at the positive emotions this creates. You will experience more joy by smiling.

16.   Accept and surrender.

It is time to stop worrying about things you cannot control. We all hear this, and we all know this intellectually, but few of us practice it. Surrender is more than just letting go; it is allowing a higher power or the power of the universe take care of things beyond our control. Acceptance is simply accepting 'what is' without wishing it were better or different. Acceptance gets you out of the denial that is keeping you locked into negativity.

17.   Live in real time.

The only time that is real is the present. The past is history and the future is a mystery – both simply live on in your mind and therefore are not real. To live in real time is to have a healthy relationship with the here and now. Many times we are so consumed by the past or the future that we can't concentrate on what we are experiencing at the moment. It is as if the past or future is robbing us of our experience. Don't wait for quality time – make now-time quality time.

18.   Take responsibility for your own emotions.

All you have to do is listen to yourself and the people around you to realize how often other people are controlling your emotions and blocking your ability to experience joy. It is not like they are standing over you preventing it, but you have let them. If you ever say, "He makes me so mad," or "I can't stand my boss; he makes me so angry," you are letting that person control your emotions. Take charge. Own your emotions. We don't take charge by changing our emotions immediately. We take charge and own our emotions by starting to change our language. Instead of "He makes me so mad," say, "I feel angry," or "I feel anxious," or "I feel"… whatever. You are not your anger, and you are certainly capable of not letting anyone control your emotions.

Chapter 29

You Are Strong!

If you could be anybody, would you be *you*? I hope that this book gives you greater confidence to answer that question with a resounding YES! This book is about rediscovering who you are from the inside out. It starts with helping you rediscover your true value and increase your self-worth using the I AM STRONG formula. There are thousands of self-help books out there by well known authors that will help you grow and become a better person, but until you spend the time to truly feel your worth, the impact will be minimized. I use the term rediscover because I sincerely believe we were born with immeasurable worth; however, through experience, training, interactions with others and life in general, we learn to devalue ourselves or look to external sources to determine our value. Your value is determined internally. Your circumstances do not define you; you are not your body, you are not your net-worth, and you are not what others say you are. Even if they say wonderful things about you, you are so much more than that. Don't fall prey to the idea that you need to be great at something in order to be of value. You are valuable because of who you are not what you do.

As you discover that you are not defined by what you do and feel the power of healthy self-worth, you are now in a position to experience the miracles of forgiving. In Part 2, you learned the powerful benefits of forgiving first yourself and then others. You may have thought you don't have anything or anyone to forgive. I assure you that you do.

By way of analogy, barnacles are a destructive organism that clings to the bottom of boats; over time the barnacles become so dense and so heavy that they add drag and weight to the boat making it unseaworthy until the barnacles are scraped off. When you don't forgive yourself and others, emotional barnacles attach themselves to you, adding drag and weight to your emotional health. Forgiving miraculously removes those emotional barnacles from your soul, enabling you to experience your self-worth, and prepares you to free yourself from past experiences, as discussed in Part 3. Holding a grudge is like holding on to a hot coal with the intention of throwing it at someone. It only ends up hurting you and robs you of the joy you can experience. Learn to be a forgiver and forgive quickly. The sooner you forgive, the more joy you will experience.

It is unfortunate that so many people carry around burdens from their past. All too often I meet people who are so weighed down by their past that they are unable to enjoy the present. You don't have to be a victim any longer. Don't let the past define who you are. Once again, it is not what happens to you that defines you. It is how you react to what happens that makes you who you are. In Part 3, you learned a valuable and powerful skill, retelling the stories that you tell yourself. This skill requires only 90 seconds to transform you from a victim of the past to a hero in your life story. By hero I mean the opposite of victim. Imagine being the hero of your own life. The words alone should be enough to motivate you to overcome your negative past and put Part 3 into action.

Living in today's world is like sailing on an ocean where the trade winds are constantly blowing us to and fro. We live in a time of great opportunity and options. In fact, there may be so many options that you feel paralyzed to determine your true purpose and path. Part 4 is dedicated to help you rediscover your true life's purpose so that you won't drift aimlessly or get tossed to and fro by the winds of life. It is important to reiterate that discovering your purpose should come after some serious attention to the first three parts in this book. Your purpose will become clearer as you grow your self-worth, forgive, and unload baggage from the past. Your purpose should not be determined by what others expect of you but by what you determine to be your path. Feeling lost, alone and directionless can create feelings of anxiety and depression. Pick a purpose to live by, set meaningful goals and strive to accomplish them. A purposeful life provides context and meaning to your daily experience and can increase your chances to experience joy on a daily basis.

Finally, the result of growing high self-worth, forgiving, overcoming the past and living with purpose is to experience joy each and every day. Joy is here right now. It is here this moment even as you read this final section. You don't have to wait for something to 'bring' you joy, or wait for the right circumstances to feel powerful and healing joy. Joy can be felt right now.

This book is meant to be a practical and powerful guide to open your eyes to your true value and help you create the strength to overcome adversity, trauma and drama. Applying the principles detailed in this book will enable you to see just how wonderful you are. You are strong! You can do both hard and amazing things. As you use the skills in this book you will begin to see the 'you' that has been inside you all this time. You are amazing, and it is now time to start living that way and experience your true purpose and potential and experience true joy.

I AM STRONG!

Bibliography

'40s Sounds Return to Radio (PDF). *Oakland Tribune,* October 29, 1972. Retrieved April 3, 2009.

Alexander, Scott W. "Generosity." River Road Unitarian Universalist Congregation. http://www.rruc.org/sermons/sermon060319.htm.

Bible, New King James Version.

Buettner, Dan. "Find Purpose, Live Longer: Add Years to your Life by Adding Life to your Years." *AARP Magazine,* November/December 2008.

Carlson, Richard. *You Can Be Happy No Matter What: Five Principles for Keeping Life in Perspective.* California: New World Library, 2006.

Emmons, R.A. and McCullough, M.E. "Counting Blessings Versus Burdens: An Experimental Investigation of Gratitude and Subjective Well-Being in Daily Life." *Journal of Personality and Social Psychology,* 84 (2). 2003.

Fedor, James H. *As a Man Thinketh,Volume 2.* Clearfield: MindArt, 2004.

Frankl, Viktor. *Man's Search for Meaning.* New York: Beacon Press, 2006.

Linley, P. A. and Joseph, S. "Positive Change Following Trauma and Adversity: A Review." *Journal of Traumatic Stress,* 17 (1) (2004).

Mack, Robert. *Happiness from the Inside Out: The Art and Science of Fulfillment.* California: New World Library, 2009.

McCullough, Michael E., et al. "Interpersonal Forgiving in Close Relationships." *Journal of Personality and Social Psychology,* 75 (6). (1998).

Pearsall, Paul. *Super Joy.* New York: Bantam, 1990.

Ramirez, E., Maldonado, A. and Martos, R. "Attribution Modulate Immunization Against Learned Helplessness in Humans." *Journal of Personality and Social Psychology,* 62. (1992).

Rand, Ayn. *Atlas Shrugged.* New York: Penguin, 2005.

Reed, Gayle L. and Enright, Robert D. "The Effects of Forgiveness Therapy on Depression, Anxiety, and Posttraumatic Stress for Women After Spousal Emotional Abuse." *Journal of Consulting and Clinical Psychology,* 74(5). (2006).

Seligman, M.E.P. *Helplessness: On Depression, Development, and Death.* San Francisco: W.H. Freeman, 1975.

Seligman, M.E.P. and Maier, S.F. "Failure to Escape Traumatic Shock." *Journal of Experimental Psychology,* 74. (1967).

Sherman, Len. *Popcorn King: How Orville Redenbacher and his Popcorn Charmed America.* City: Summit Group, 1996.

Stipek, D. E. P. *Motivation to Learning.* Boston: Allyn & Bacon, 1988.

Sutton, Geoffrey W. and Allman, Jaimee. "Forgiveness, Reconciliation, and Spirituality: Empirical Findings Regarding Conceptual Differences." Paper presented at the annual meeting of the Christian Association of Psychological Studies, Orlando, Florida, 2009.

Swift, Brad. *Life on Purpose, Six Passages to an Inspired Life.* California: Elite Books, 2007.

Swindoll, Charles. *The Ragged Edge.* Nashville: Thomas Nelson, 2004.

Tedeshi, R.G., Calhoon, L.G. and Cann, A. "Evaluating Resource Gain: Understanding and Misunderstanding Posttraumatic Growth." *Applied Psychology: An International Review,* 56 (3) (2007).

Val, E. B. and Linley, P. A., "Posttraumatic Growth, Positive Changes, and Negative Changes in Madrid Residents Following the March 11, 2004, Madrid Train Bombings." *Journal of Loss and Trauma,* 11. (2006).

Weiss, T. "Posttraumatic Growth in Women with Breast Cancer and Their Husbands: An Intersubjective Validation Study." *Journal of Psychosocial Oncology,* 20. (2002).

Wilkinson, Kirk. *The Happiness Factor: How to Be Happy No Matter What!* Austin: Ovation, 2008.

Worthington, Everett L., Jr. and Scherer, Michael. "Forgiveness is an Emotion-Focused Coping Strategy that can Reduce Health Risks and Promote Health Resilience: Theory, Review, and Hypotheses." *Psychology and Health,* 19. (2004).

I AM STRONG!

Endnotes

1   Linley and Joseph, "Positive Change Following Trauma and Adversity: A Review," 11-21; Tedeshi, Calhoon, and Cann, "Evaluating Resource Gain: Understanding and Misunderstanding Posttraumatic Growth," 396; Val and Linley, "Posttraumatic Growth, Positive Changes, and Negative Changes in Madrid Residents Following the March 11, 2004, Madrid Train Bombings," 409-424; Weiss, "Posttraumatic Growth in Women with Breast Cancer and Their Husbands: An Intersubjective Validation Study," 65-80.

2   Fedor, *As a Man Thinketh,Volume 2*, 5.

3   Carlson, *You Can Be Happy No Matter What: Five Principles for Keeping Life in Perspective*, 12.

4   Swindoll, *The Ragged Edge*, 39.

5   Bible, John 8:32.

6   Wilkinson, *The Happiness Factor: How to Be Happy No Matter What!*, 53.

7   Worthington and Scherer, "Forgiveness is an Emotion-Focused Coping Strategy that can Reduce Health Risks and Promote Health Resilience: Theory, Review, and Hypotheses," 385-405.

8   Sutton and Allman. "Forgiveness, Reconciliation, and Spirituality: Empirical Findings Regarding Conceptual Differences."

9   www.forgiving.org.

10   Reed and Enright, "The Effects of Forgiveness Therapy on Depression, Anxiety, and Posttraumatic Stress for Women After Spousal Emotional Abuse," 920-929.

11   McCullough, et al, "Interpersonal Forgiving in Close Relationships," 1586-1603.

12   Seligman and Maier, "Failure to Escape Traumatic Shock," 1–9; Seligman, *Helplessness: On Depression, Development, and Death.*

13   Ramirez, Maldonado and Martos, "Attribution Modulate Immunization Against Learned Helplessness in Humans," 139-146.

14   Sherman, *Popcorn King: How Orville Redenbacher and his Popcorn Charmed America,* 49.

15   Mack, *Happiness from the Inside Out: The Art and Science of Fulfillment,* 122.

16   Frankl, *Man's Search for Meaning,* 9.

17   Rand , *Atlas Shrugged,* 99.

18   Swift, *Life on Purpose, Six Passages to an Inspired Life,* 85.

19   Buettner, "Find Purpose, Live Longer: Add Years to your Life by Adding Life to your Years."

20 Emmons and McCullough, "Counting Blessings Versus Burdens: An Experimental Investigation of Gratitude and Subjective Well-Being in Daily Life," 377–389.

21 *'40s Sounds Return to Radio* (PDF).

22 Alexander, "Generosity."

23 Pearsall, *Super Joy*, 84.

I AM STRONG!

CPSIA information can be obtained at www.ICGtesting.com
Printed in the USA
BVOW04s1245221213

339777BV00005B/20/P